Published by **PALLAS ATHENE (PUBLISHERS) LTD.** 2 Birch Close, London N19 5XD
pallasathene.co.uk

ISBN 9781843682080

Front Cover Image **MICK** ST PAUL'S CHURCH, COVENT GARDEN
Rear Cover Image **ANON** BRIDGE PLACE

Images © 2021 **ANTHONY DAWTON**
Introduction © 2021 **LEILANI FARHA**

All Photography **ANTHONY DAWTON**
dawton.com

Design & Art Direction **ROSS WHITE**
Whyt whytstudio.com

Printed in England by **JUMP DP**
jumpdp.com

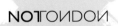

NOTONDON

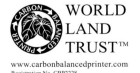

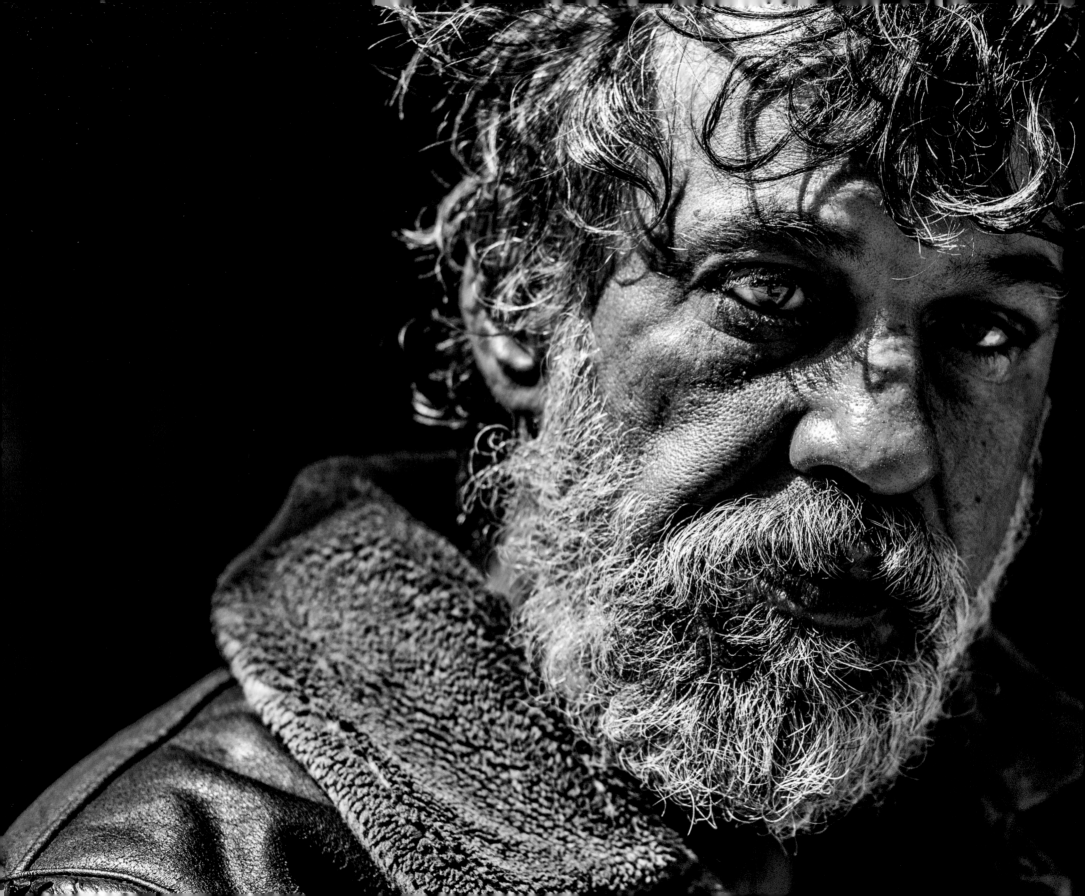

ALL HUMAN BEINGS ARE BORN FREE AND EQUAL IN DIGNITY AND RIGHTS.
Universal Declaration of Human Rights (Article 1, 1948)

I have met with homeless people in cities across the globe. On sidewalks in San Francisco and Delhi; under bridges in Paris and Lagos; in parks in Valparaiso and Belgrade; in tents in Los Angeles and Vancouver; in shelters in Barcelona and London; in abandoned buildings in Mexico City and even cars in San Diego. Each encounter was as powerful as the one before.

I was appointed United Nations Special Rapporteur on adequate housing in 2014, a post I held until 2020. For six years I was the world's top watch dog, charged with investigating housing conditions across the globe and holding governments accountable to their human rights commitments under the Universal Declaration of Human Rights, and the many international human rights treaties they have signed which protect housing as a human right.

These commitments are well-defined: as members of the human family, we each have the right to life, security of the person, and to an adequate standard of living including adequate housing, food, water and sanitation. All of which are required for human dignity – the essence of all human rights.

It quickly became clear to me that where housing is concerned, the world was in a mess – all the signs of a global housing crisis, as serious and as pressing as the climate crisis, were graffitied on the wall. They still are. Unaffordability, evictions, lack of social housing, discrimination and worst of all: growing homelessness, especially in the most affluent countries. All of which suggests governments are not abiding by their international human rights law obligations, and are doing so with impunity.

To solve a problem you need to understand that problem. Where human rights practice is concerned, you go to the source – those whose rights are most at risk. I needed to talk with people in their homes, wherever those homes happen to be. I made it my opportunity to meet those living in homelessness in all my travels. Those were my most cherished conversations – ones I will carry with me. Regardless of the city and its relative affluence, the geographic location, the weather – there were patterns and shared experiences.

Warm greetings. I am offered to stay and talk for a bit, a sip of juice, a biscuit, something procured out of nothing. One man washes his hands with bottled water before shaking mine; a woman plucks her eyebrows and puts her lipstick on outside the tent where she lives; another shows me her spotless space, adorned with a battered family photo. Each seemingly acutely aware that what holds them together, what defines them, is their dignity, under constant threat, hanging by a thread. No lavatories. No showers. No beds. No roof.

I am told stories of despair, of lack, of wanting, of violence, of cruelty, of loss and of abandonment – their experiences etched in their eyes, their teeth, their hands, their skin. They say to me: 'I just want to be treated like a human being'.

When I look up from the destitution and deprivation of lives lived on sidewalks, bridges, and parks, I see billboards advertising new luxury lifestyle apartments, cranes hovering over glass and steel skyscrapers, tall buildings with no occupants, tourists rolling suitcases to their short-term rentals.

I tell the people I meet that I can't change their individual circumstances, it's not my job. I talk to governments to influence them to think differently and from there to do more, to do better. Homeless people tell me that I am the first one with power or privilege to listen. They want to be seen. They want to be heard. I am a witness to their existence. And in the absence of spaces and places for them to speak to authorities, they want me to retell their needs (not their stories) to those who have abandoned them, to help make them visible to those who prefer not to see.

They are not victims. They are human rights defenders. Every tent erected, sleeping bag rolled out, toilet constructed is a claim: a distilled, human rights claim for survival and dignity. Cognizant that their living conditions are not acceptable, understanding they are part of a global trend, wanting their governments held accountable.

Each conversation provides me with a more finely tuned, crisp picture of our times.

I have had many meetings with government officials. They are not proud of the rising homelessness they see in their cities. Sometimes, they even express a flicker of embarrassment, which is then covered over by a rash of numbers: money spent, units built, supports provided. And yet, there is growing homelessness, I say.

I am struck by the numbers they don't talk about. The number of billionaires and amount of corporate wealth within their borders. The amount of money that flows across their borders, never to return. The money they give away on tax breaks for those who can buy the know-how to navigate the system.

They don't admit to the political and legislative energy they pour into wealth creation and maximization, shutting out those who don't fit their economic equations. They don't concede that the race for accumulation that they facilitate and foster, and the extraction of profit from every square metre of land and property, pushes people out of their homes. They choose not to make the connection between on the one hand, sidling up to corporations and on the other, the growing number of people living in homelessness.

And then, when homeless people do what's necessary to survive, governments criminalize, blame, stereotype, silence and shutter them in shelters, rooming houses, prisons. It is double jeopardy: governments create homelessness and then punish people for their homelessness. There is only one way forward. By embracing homeless people as valued members of the human family. And in this way, to make visible the invisible. In whatever way we can.

I have started a global movement, The Shift, to change how we think about homelessness, to expose and confront the systems and structures created by governments that deny people security, that push people out of their homes and communities.

I see in Anthony Dawton's confronting, haunting photographs, this making visible of the invisible, capturing the unbearable hardship of a life of homelessness, while reflecting that each homeless person is just that: a human being with inherent dignity, struggling to survive.

LEILANI FARHA
Global Director, The Shift
Former UN Special Rapporteur on the Right to Housing (2014 - 2020)
March 2021

INTRODUCTION

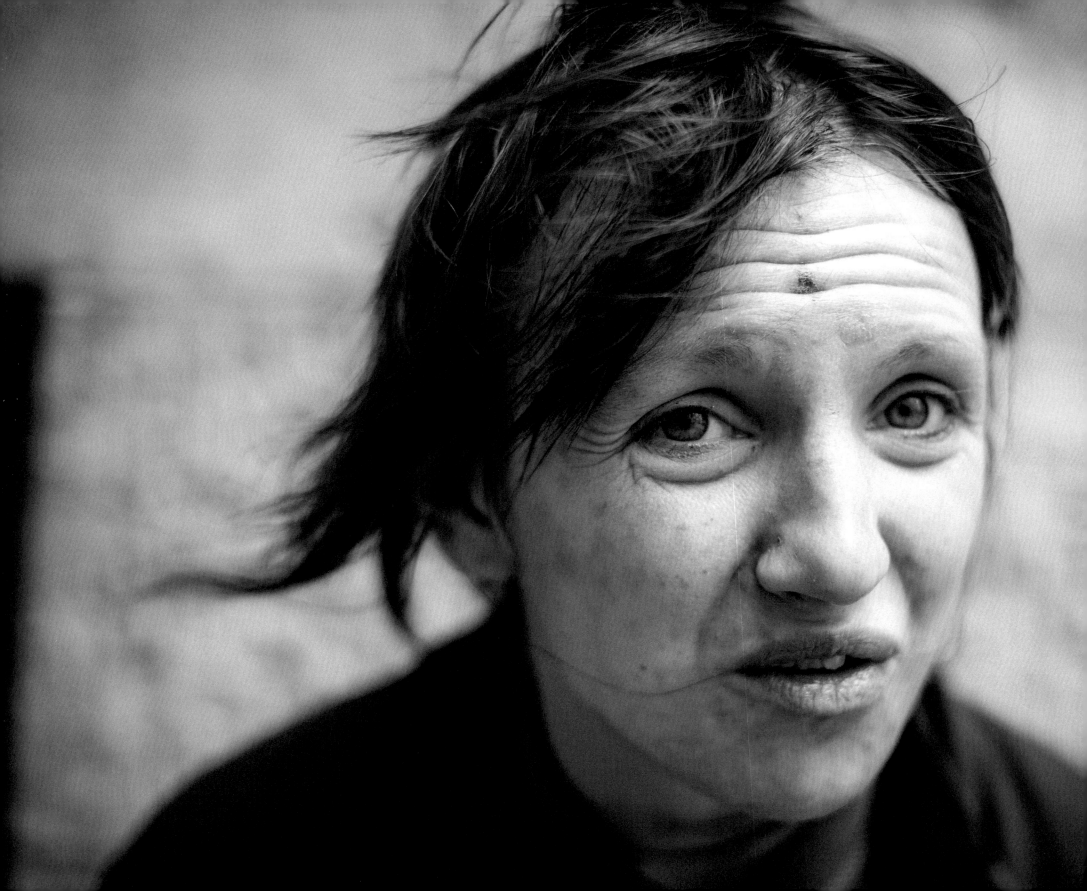

I have worked in some of the poorest countries in the world, in some of the largest refugee camps in the Middle East and other disaster areas. The misery and dangers of day-to-day life in these places, where living has been reduced to below the minimum required to maintain any dignity and self-respect, is shocking.

I would return from these trips shaken and upset but pleased to be back in London to recharge my batteries. Except, increasingly out of the corner of my eye, I was seeing a street life I had not noticed before. Thousands of people were living on the streets as damaged, scarred, hungry and as far away from their homes, as any of the refugees I had encountered on my work overseas.

In this virtually hidden place beyond the periphery of most Londoner's vision is a **NOTLONDON** of homeless people of every age and background, in doorways, under arches, in Underground stations, covered in cardboard boxes and thin blankets, and if you know where to look in the evening, in queues on the back streets of central London waiting for open-air kitchens to give them their only meal of the day.

It's as though there is a conspiracy not to see these people and yet they are there, in their thousands, on London's busiest and wealthiest streets just out of sight, a whole city of homeless people, nearly a parallel dimension, searching out the best spots to beg and sleep, anxious about where their next alcohol or drug fix is coming from and hoping hyperthermia will not claim them in the night.

If you sit on the pavement with them, they readily engage you in conversation. It is rare, they tell you, that anyone talks to them. The narratives that have reduced them to living on the streets are usually of abandoned or abused childhoods. Of mothers and fathers whom they never knew or at least never knew sober. Or they are stories of heartbreak and betrayal, frequently the stories of the younger homeless. They are lonely, often scarred and tragically too ashamed to return to families that would welcome them back. **NOTLONDON** is a tragic, precarious and dangerous place.

I would return a few days later to give them a copy of their photograph. Sometimes they were still there, sometimes their colleagues simply told me they had gone away or, all too frequently, that they had died, usually from hyperthermia, drugs or any number of underlying health problems. But gone away or dead, their 'spots' were quickly occupied.

ANTHONY DAWTON
February 2021

I must acknowledge those who helped and supported me throughout the **NOTLONDON** project:

HENRI KISELEWSKI whose constant advice has given this project direction, confidence and integrity. BILLY DAWTON for his support and for building the on-line presence for the project. To ROSS WHITE who although came late to the project managed to 'art direct' the project in reverse and give my photographs the elegance and a narrative that seems to me close to magic. LOUISA MACMILLLAN for her generous support and her always kind and incisive advice. To DIA AZZAWI for his support and who taught me that nothing beautiful can be created without commitment. LEILANI FARHA for anchoring the book with her wonderful introduction. To DAVID ELLIOTT for his skill and wisdom and lastly to RICHARD CURRALL who as fate would have it, met me on the very first day I began the **NOTLONDON** project and who has been with me for the entire duration. Without him none of this would have happened.

WHERE IS NOT LONDON?

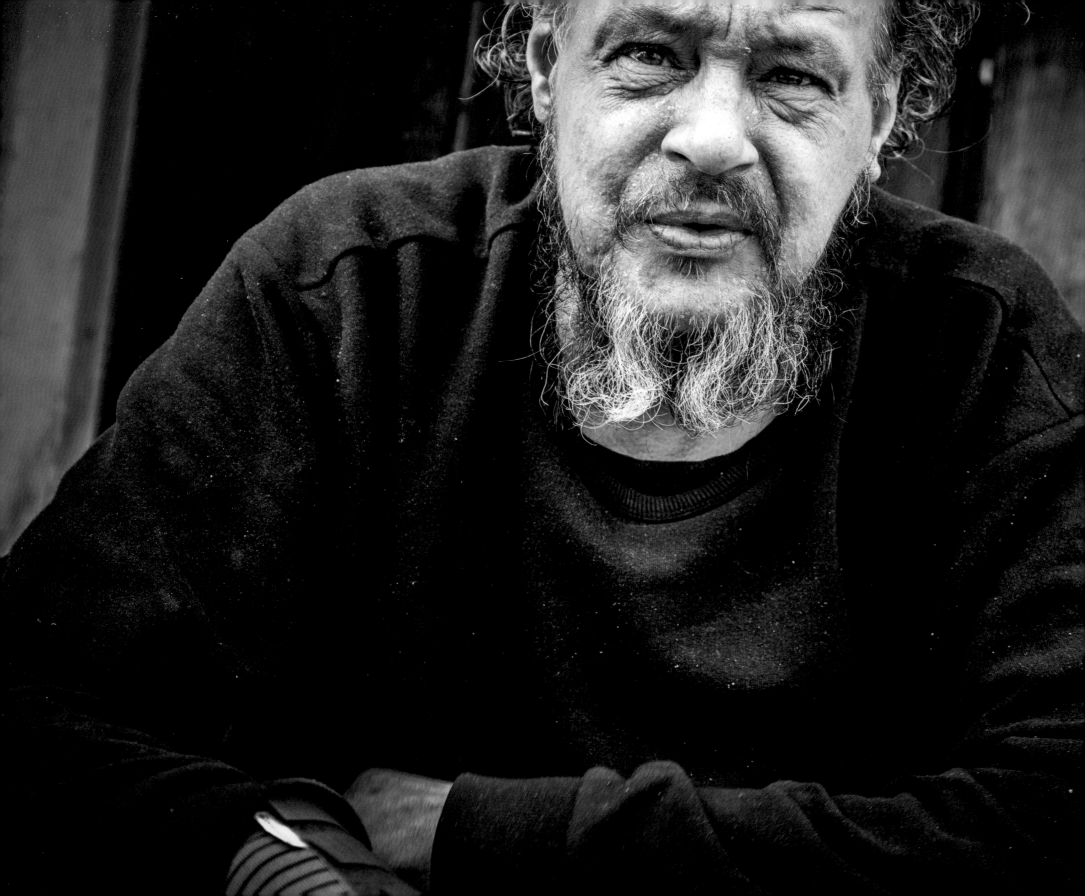

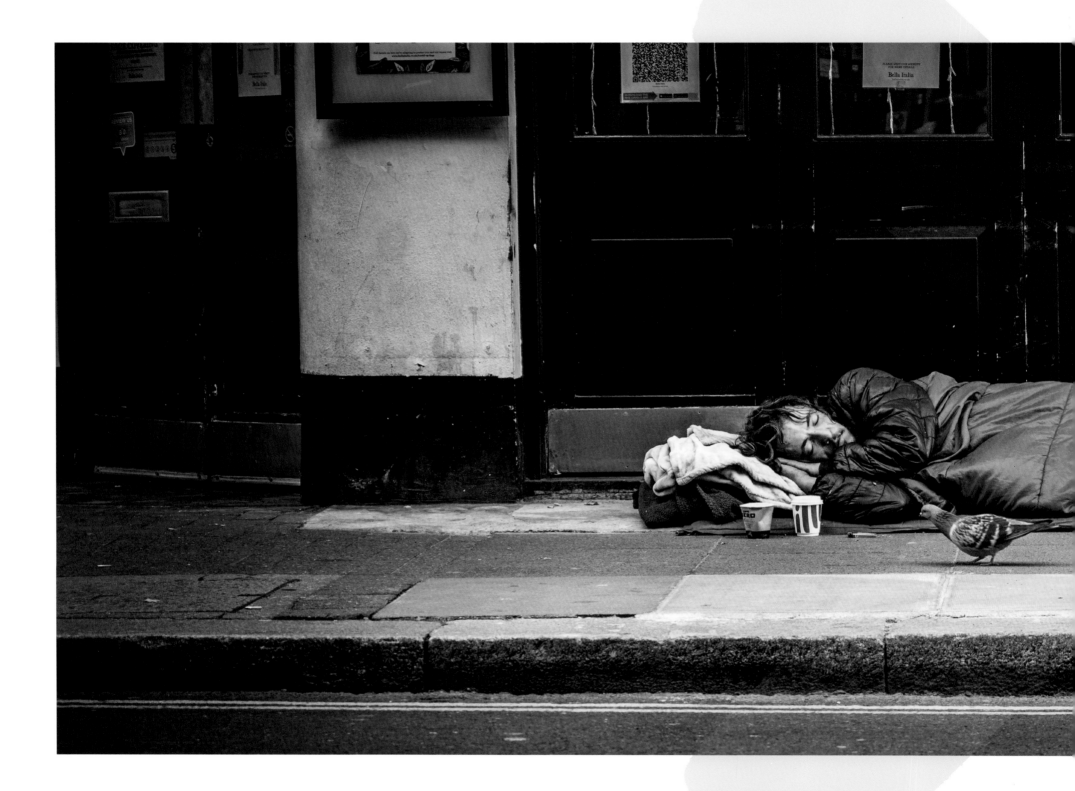

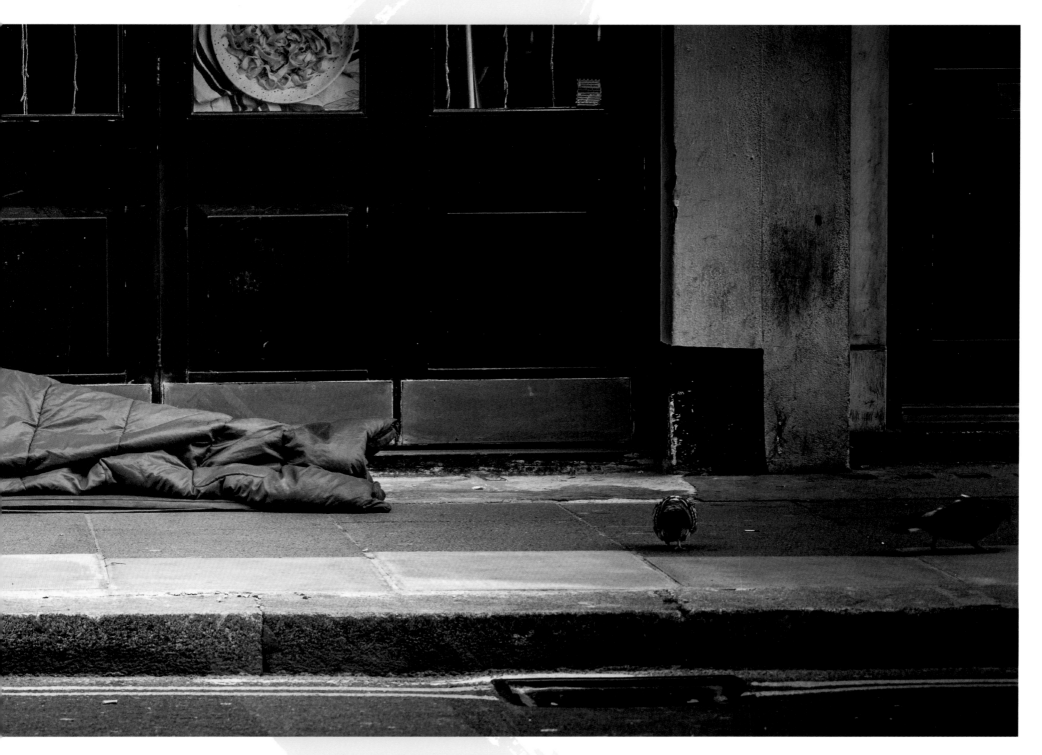

<< **VINCENT** OLD BROMPTON ROAD / **AMY (& FLEUR)** CHARING CROSS ROAD >

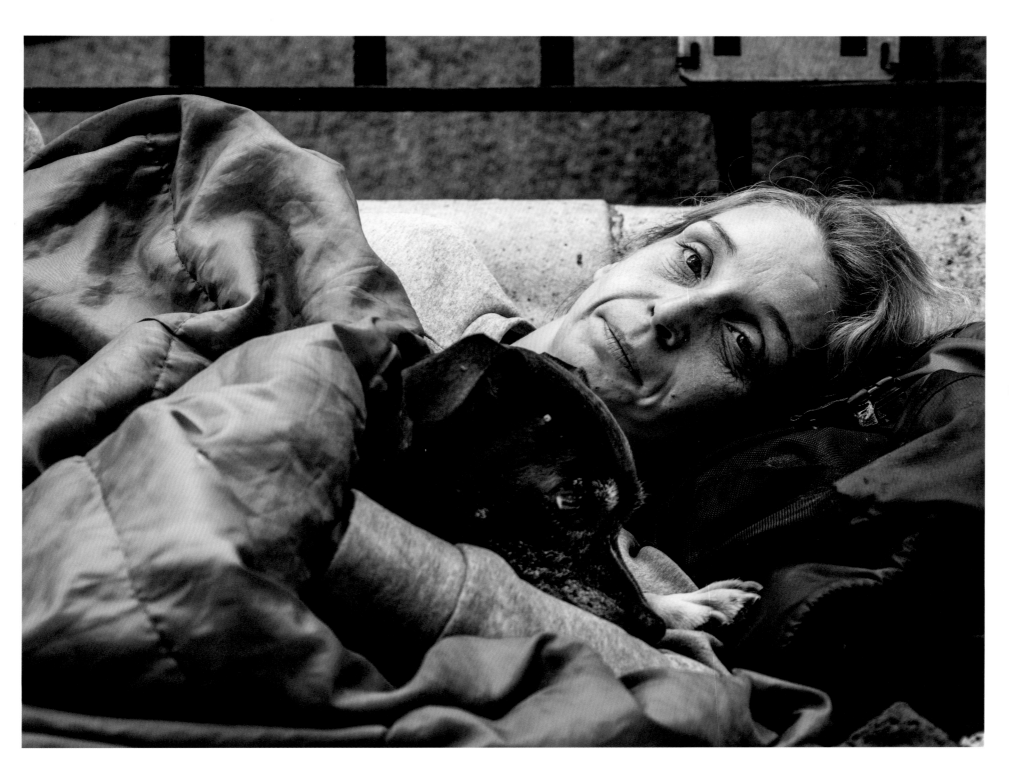

MARIE VICTORIA STATION

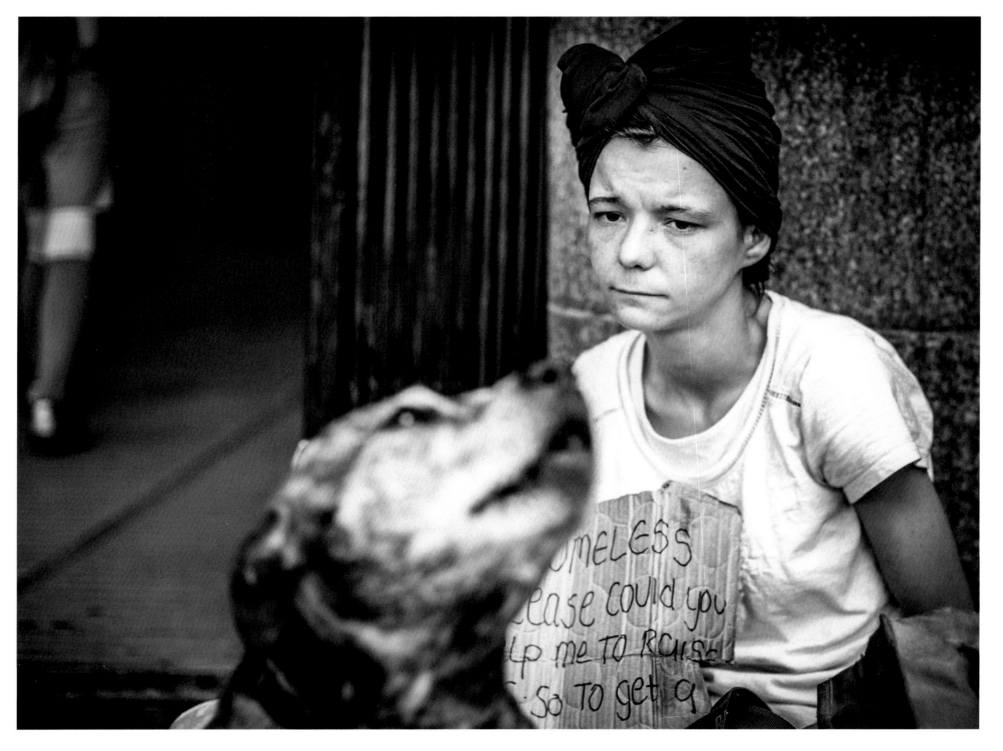

'PRE-RAPHAELITE' CHRISTOPHER GARDENS

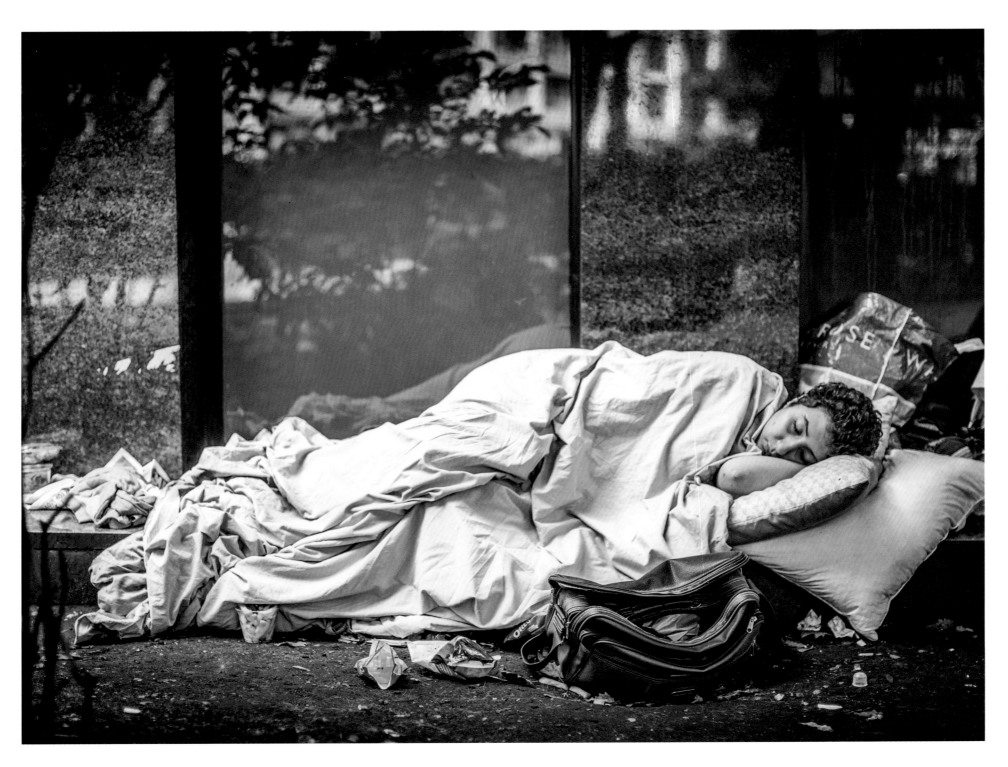

BEN CHARING CROSS ROAD

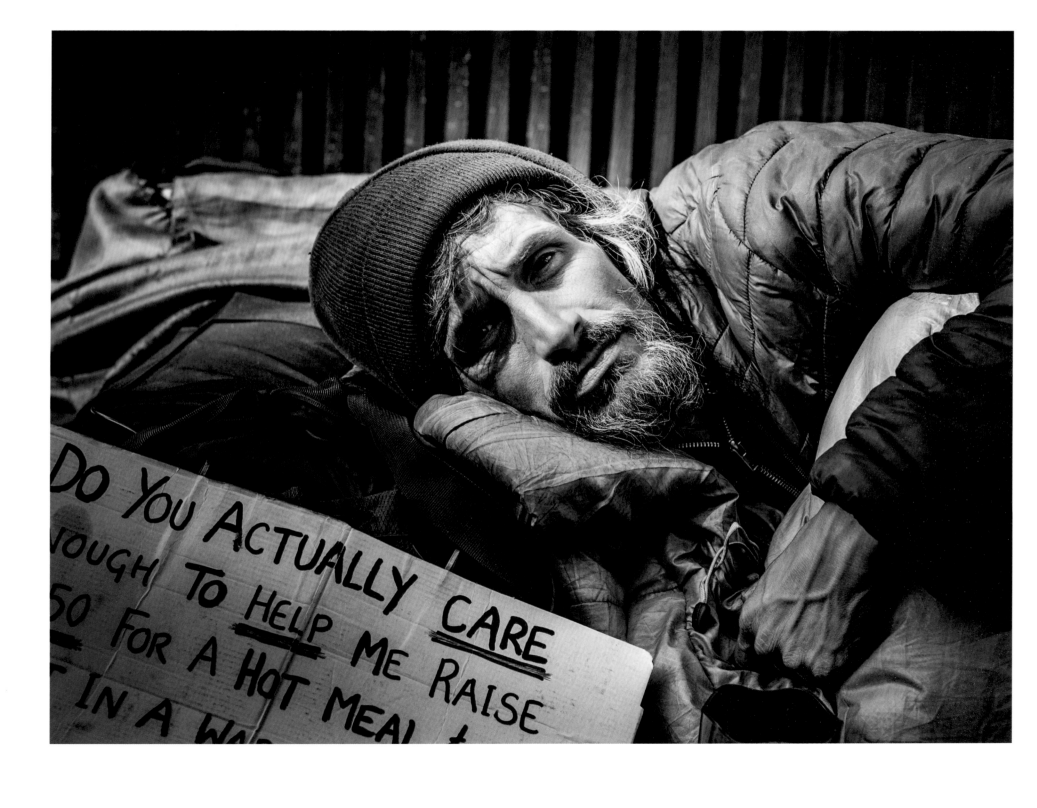

KINGSLEY CHRISTOPHER GARDENS

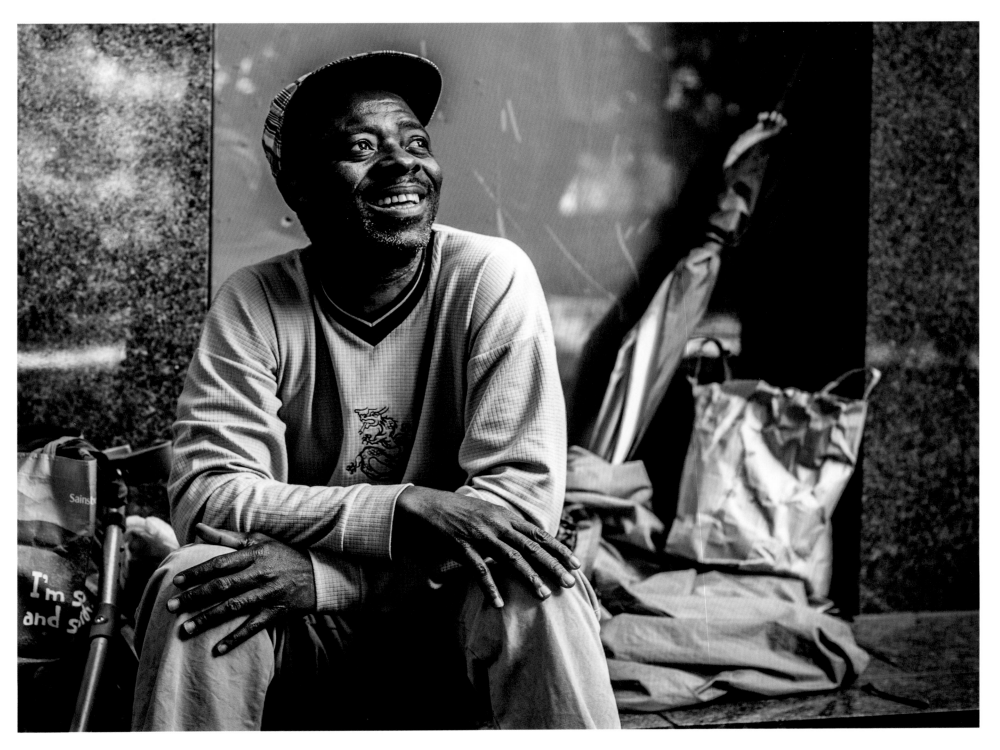

ANON DEAN STREET

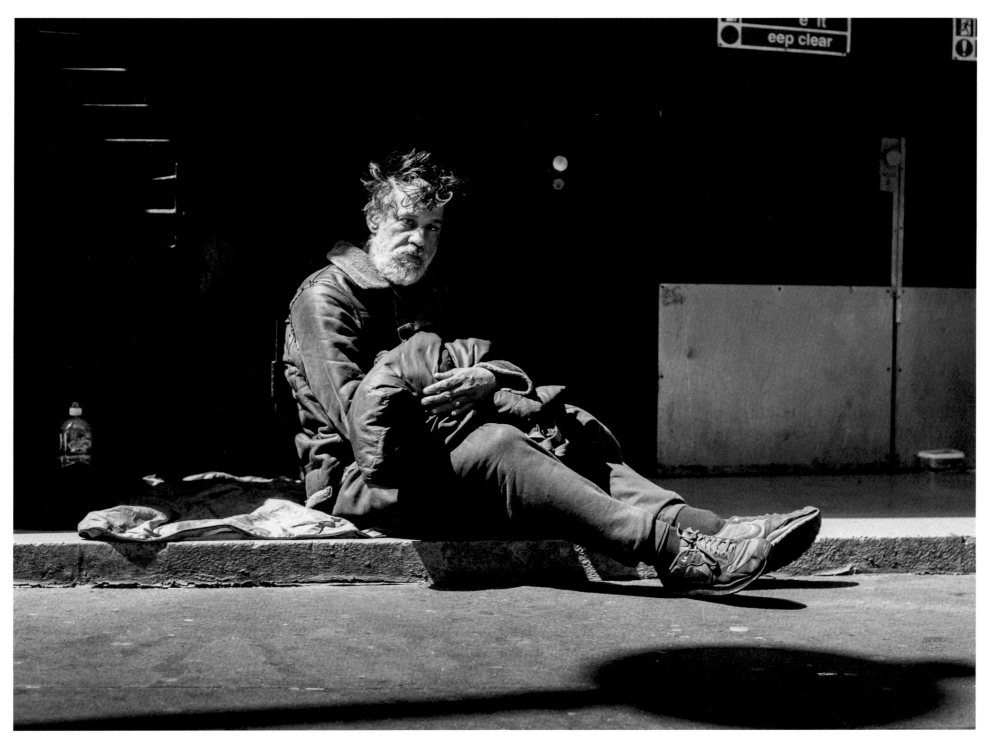

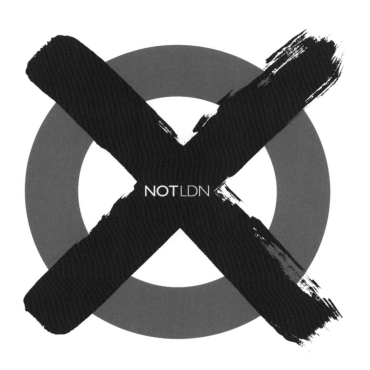

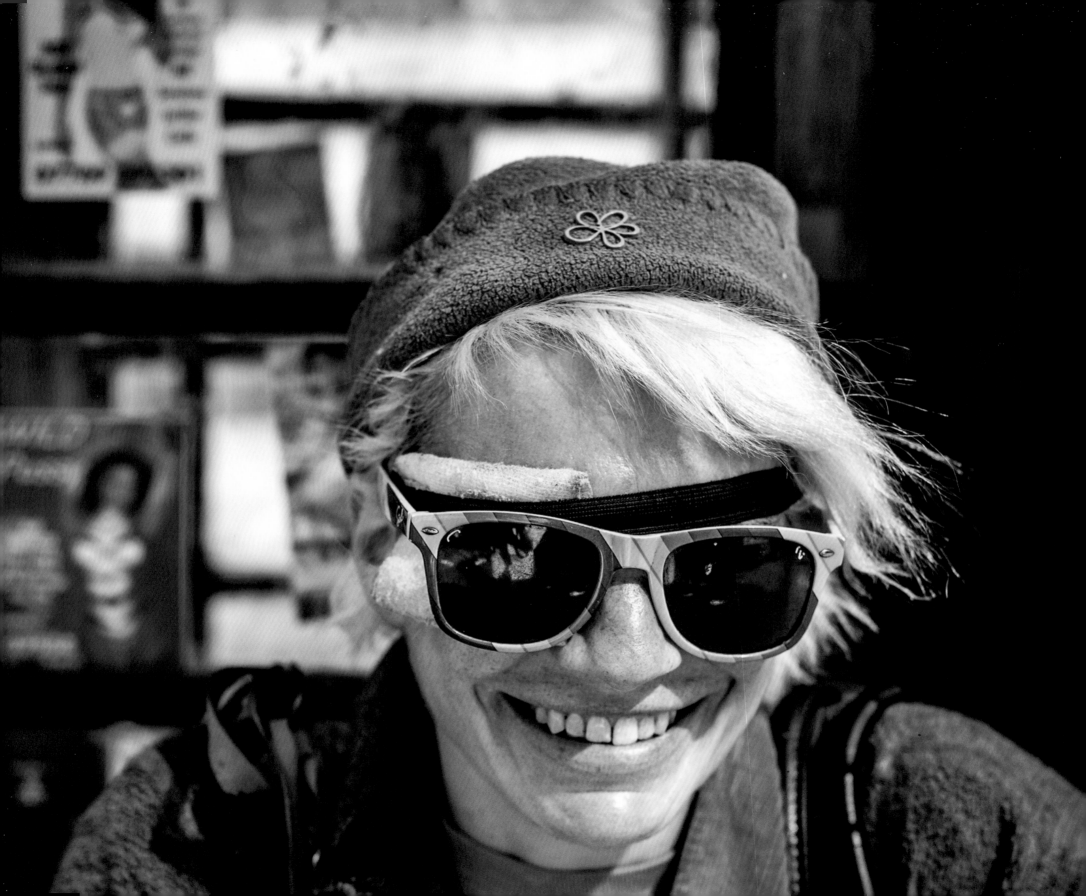

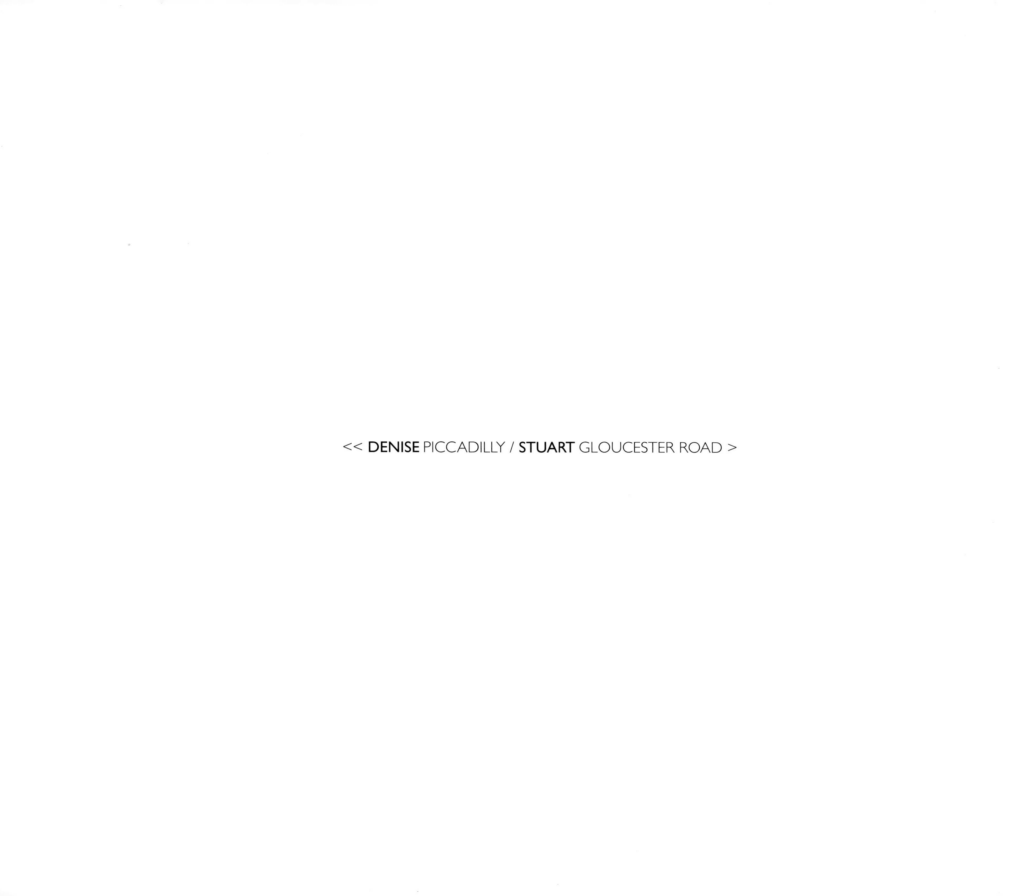

<< **DENISE** PICCADILLY / **STUART** GLOUCESTER ROAD >

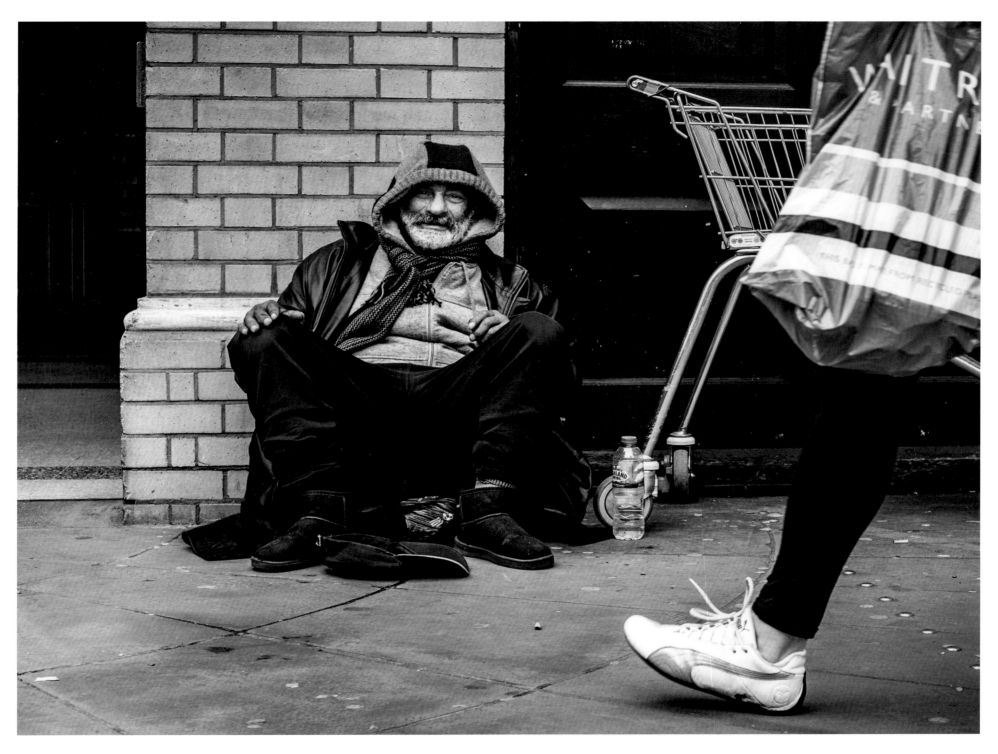

ANON CHRISTOPHER GARDENS

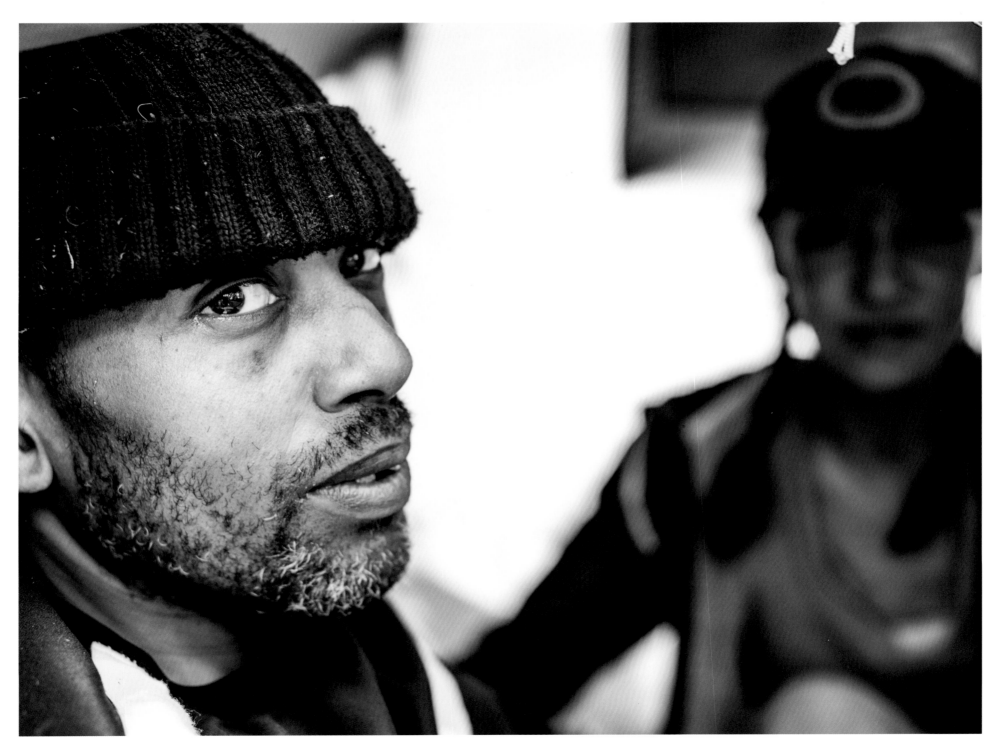

MARK VICTORIA

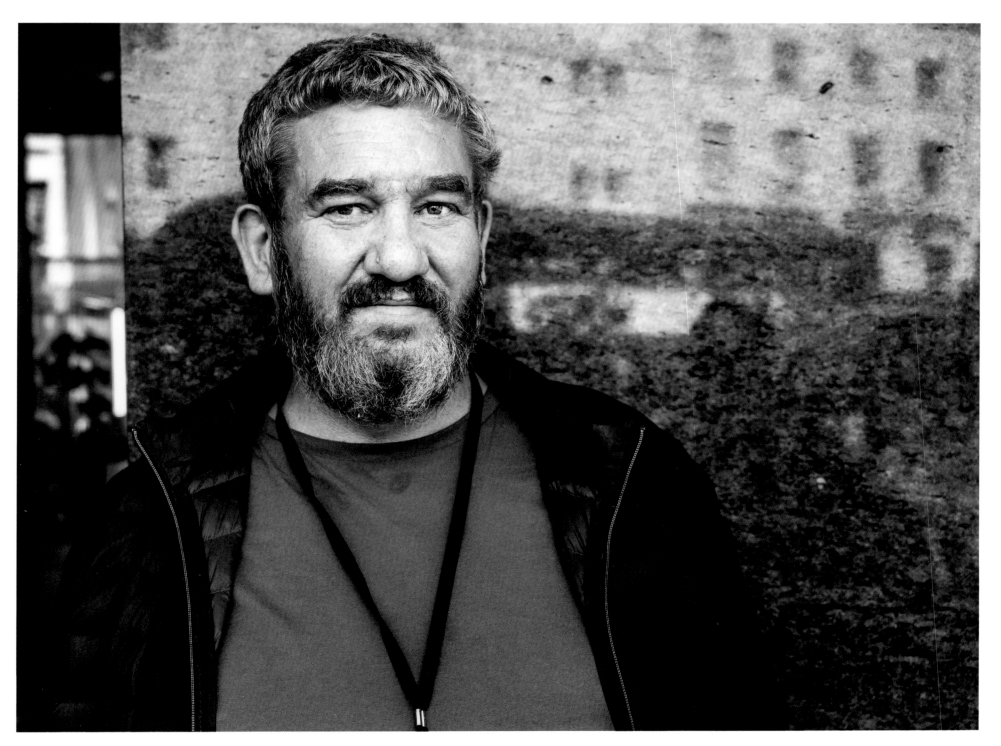

DEAN & HAYLEY VAUXHALL BRIDGE ROAD

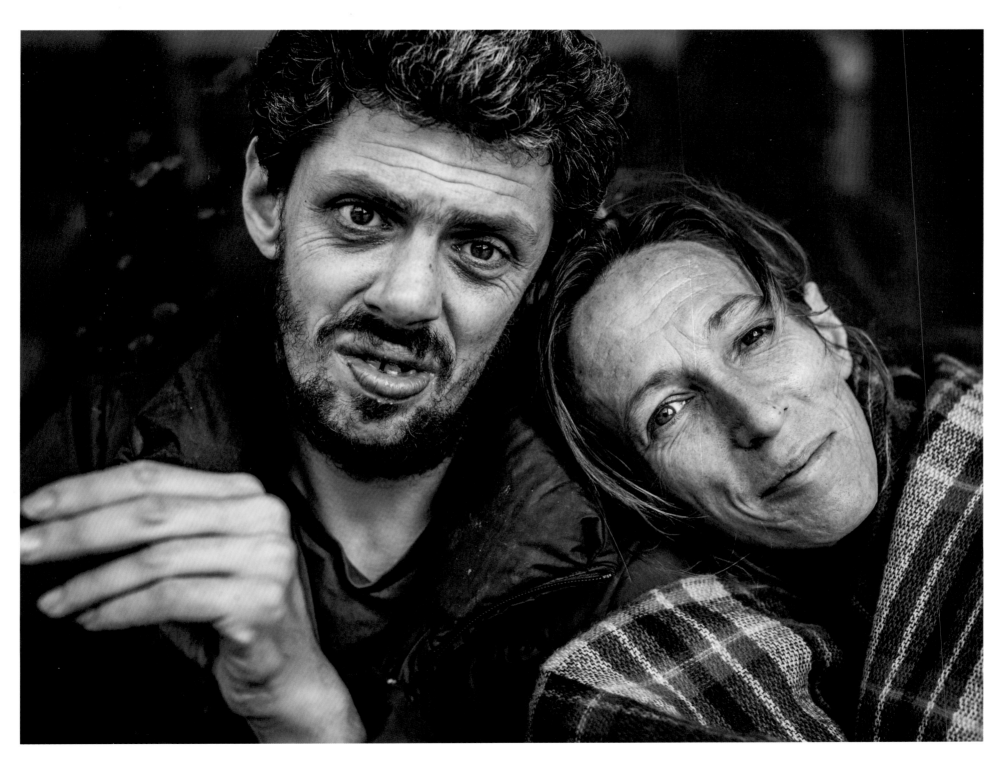

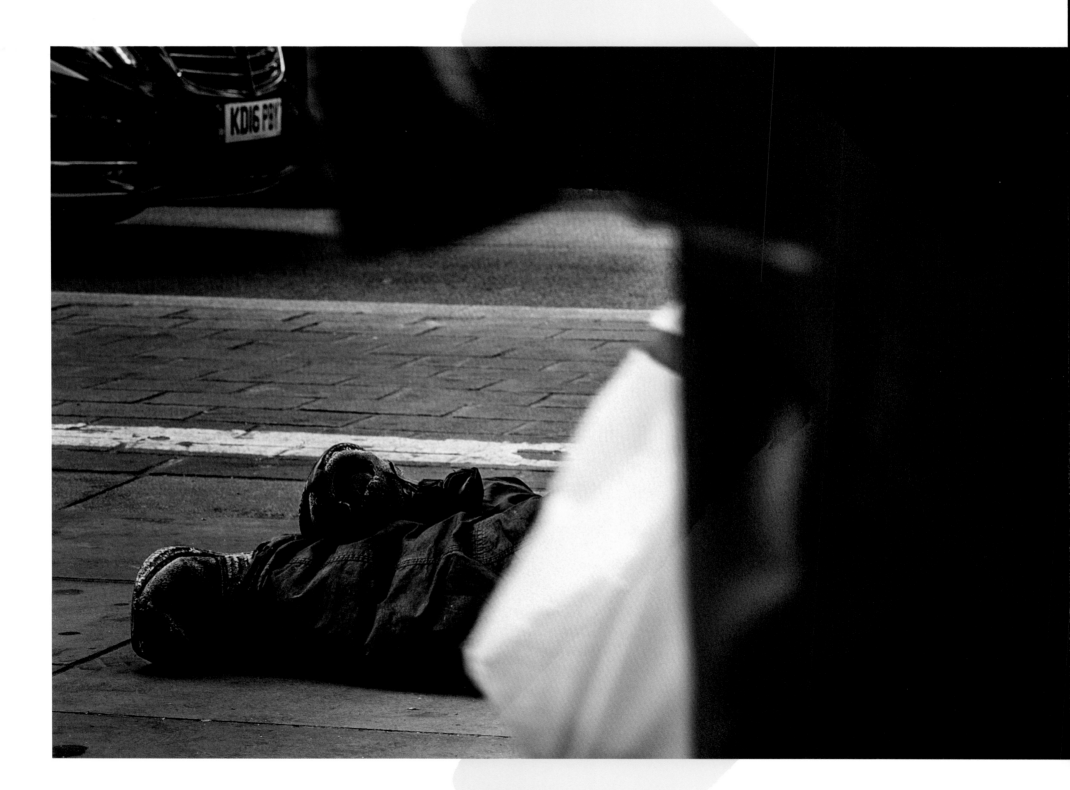

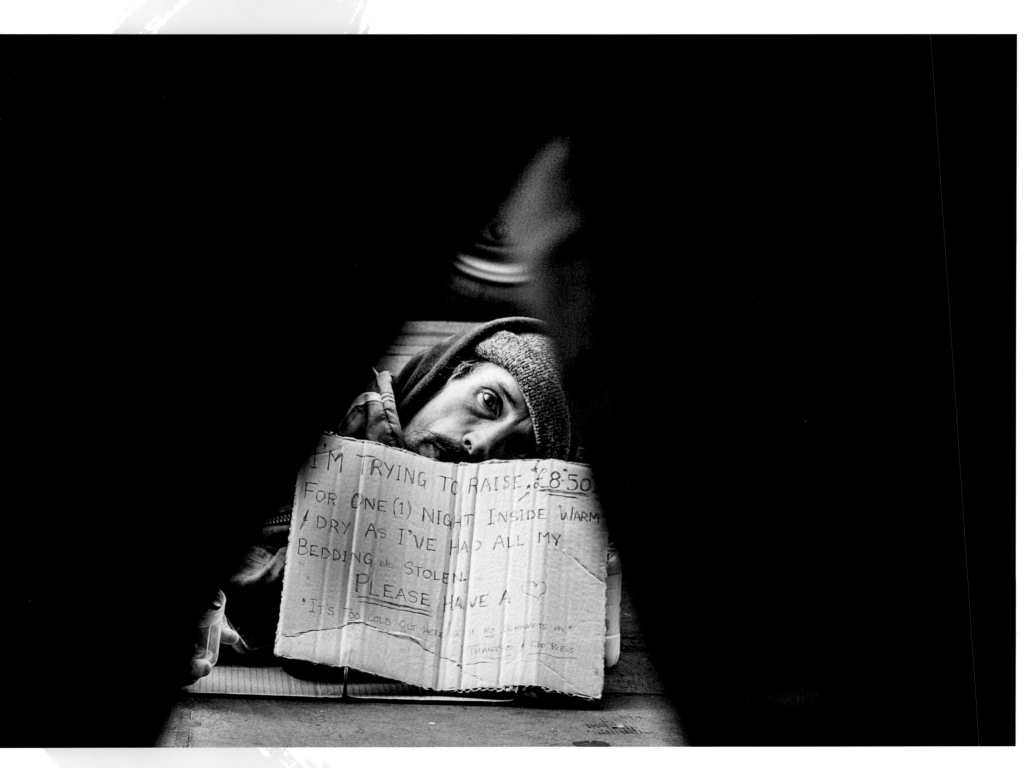

<< **ANON** LEICESTER SQUARE / **ANON** CHARING CROSS ROAD >

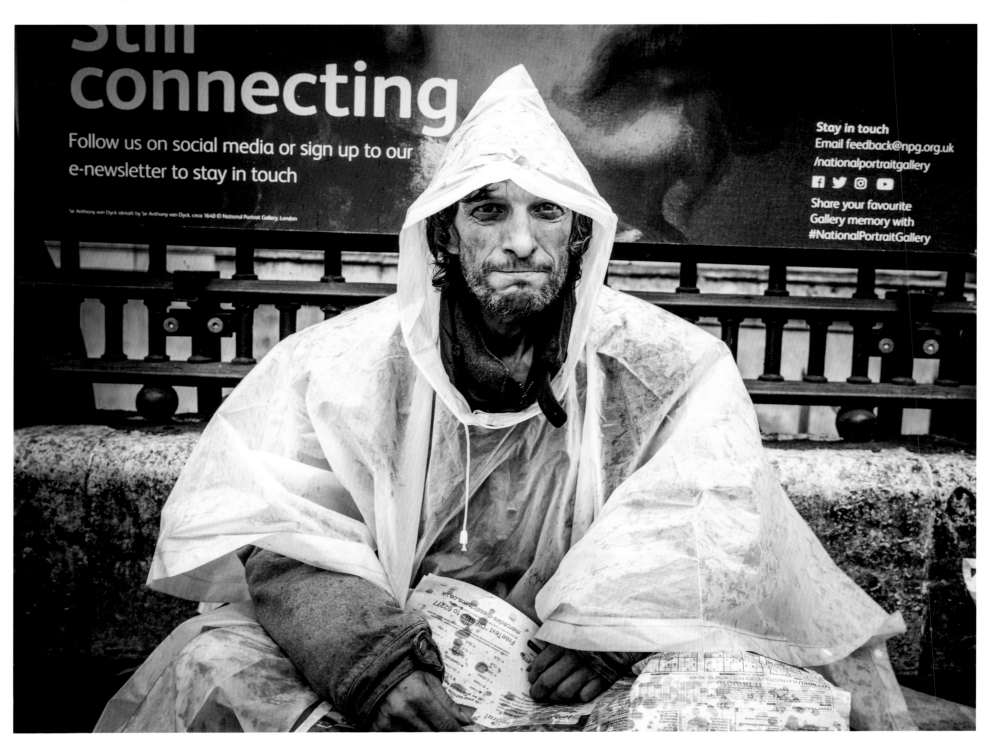

REBECCA SOUTH KENSINGTON STATION ARCADE

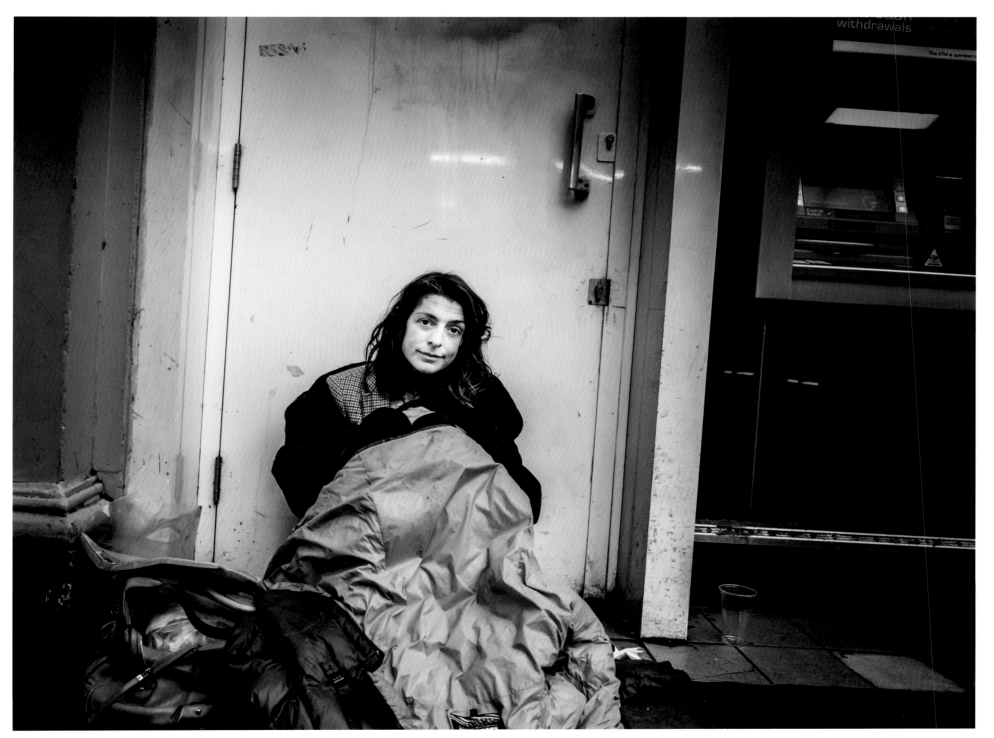

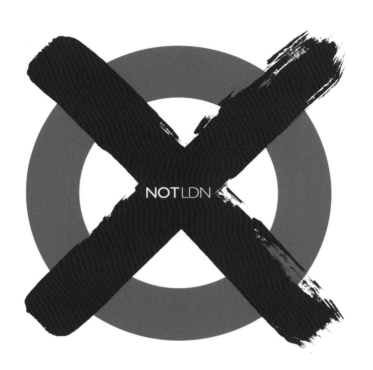

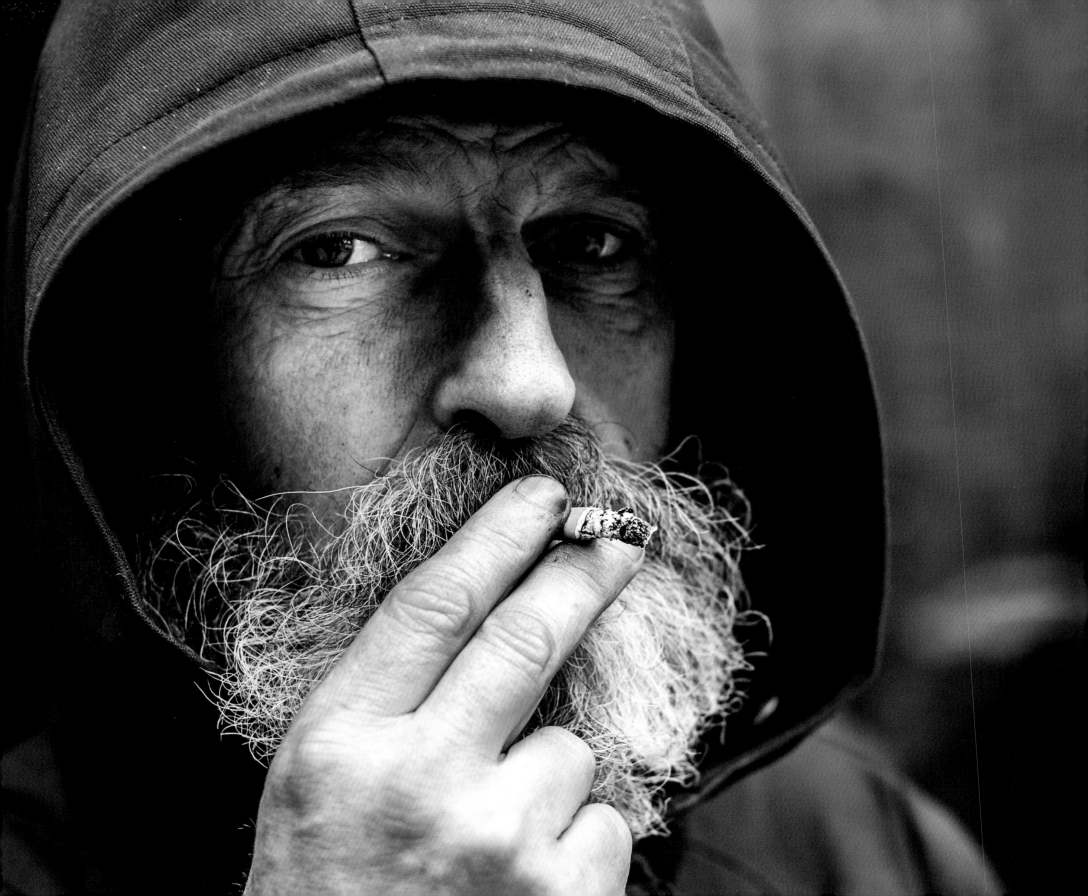

<< **ANON** ASHLEY PLACE / **GARY** ASHLEY PLACE >

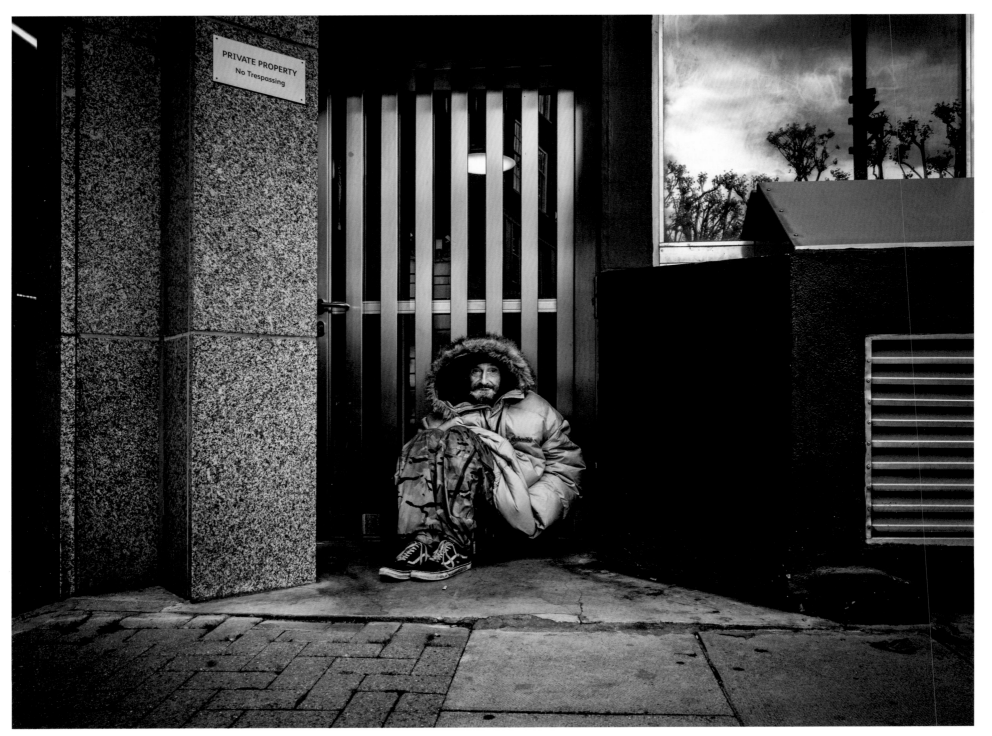

JOVITA & MARCO CHRISTOPHER GARDENS

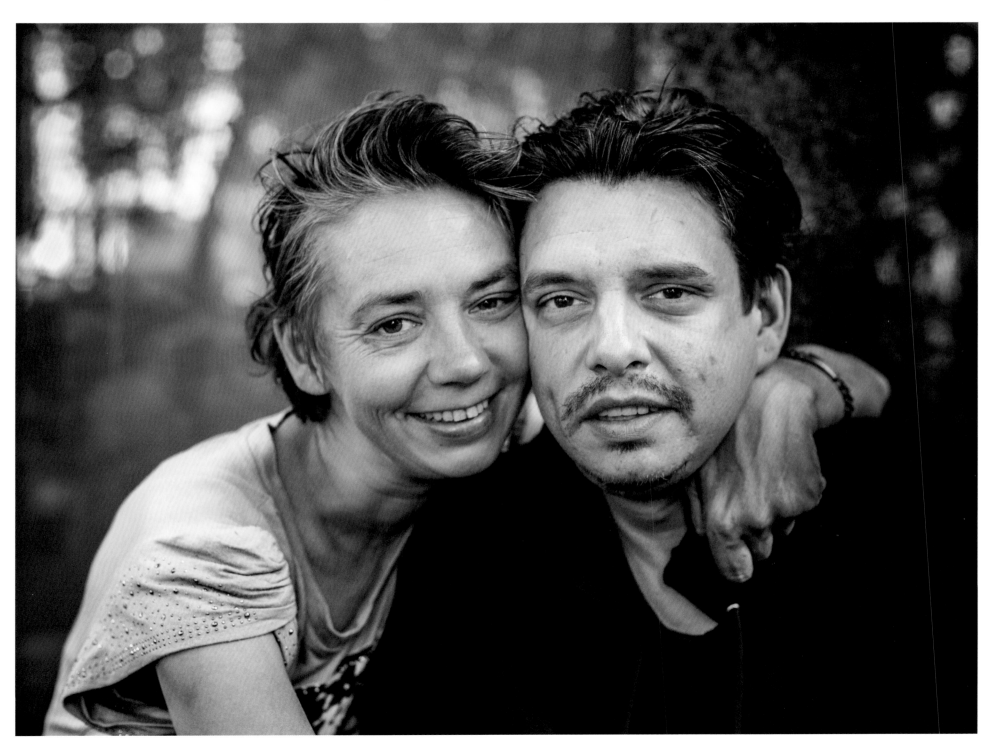

ANON VICTORIA STREET

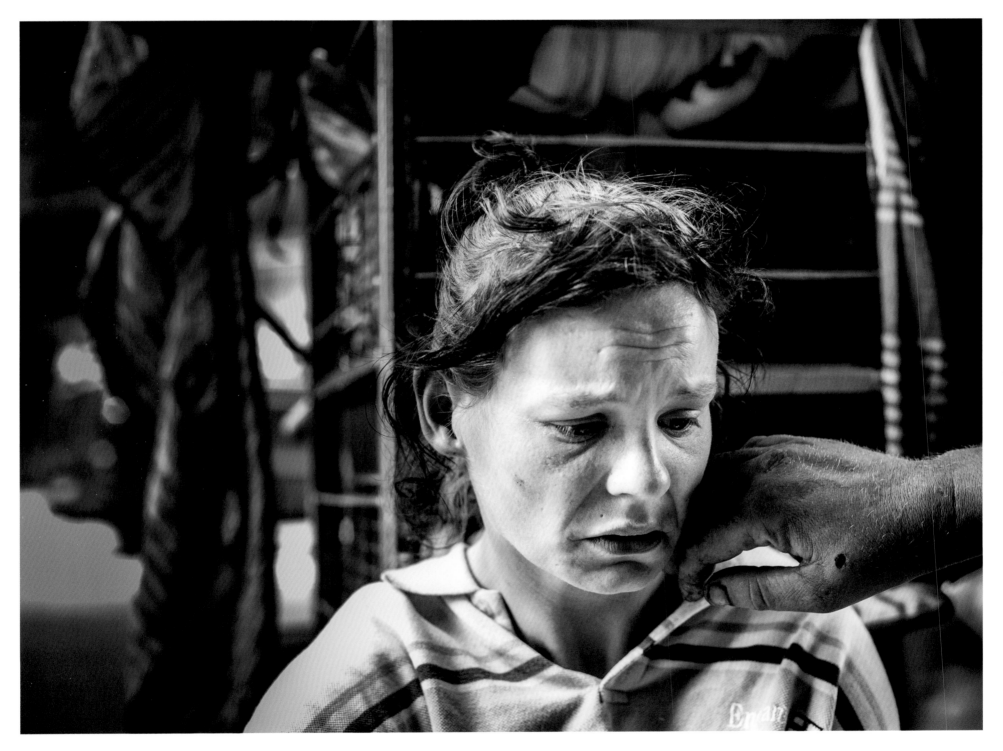

"GOD BLESS" PICCADILLY

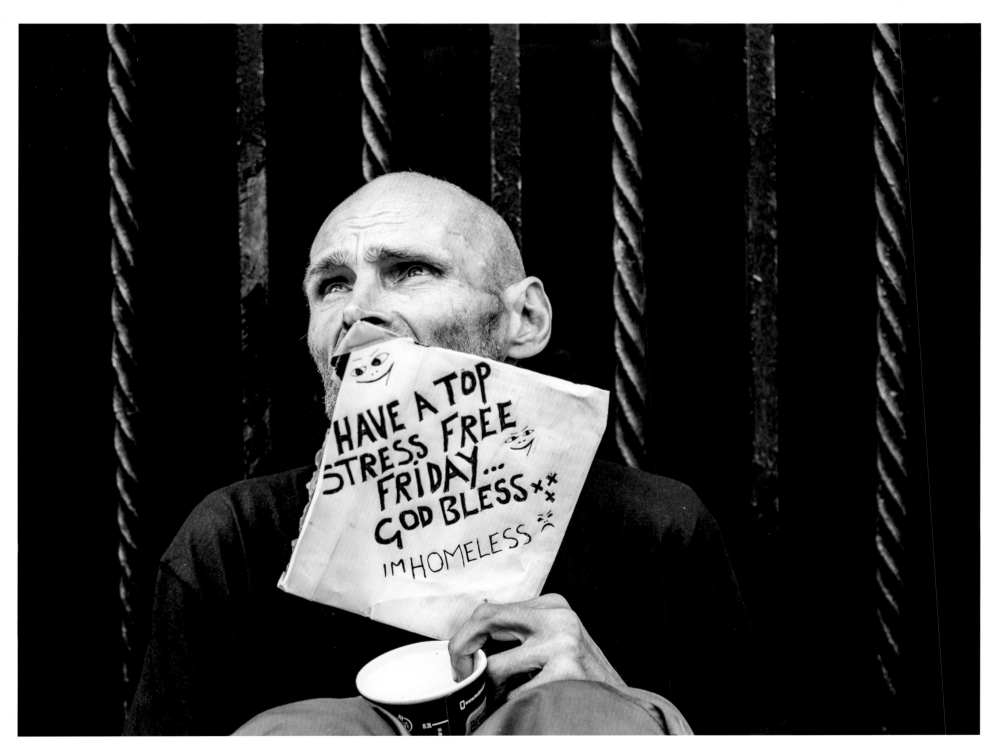

JAMES SOUTH KENSINGTON TUBE STATION

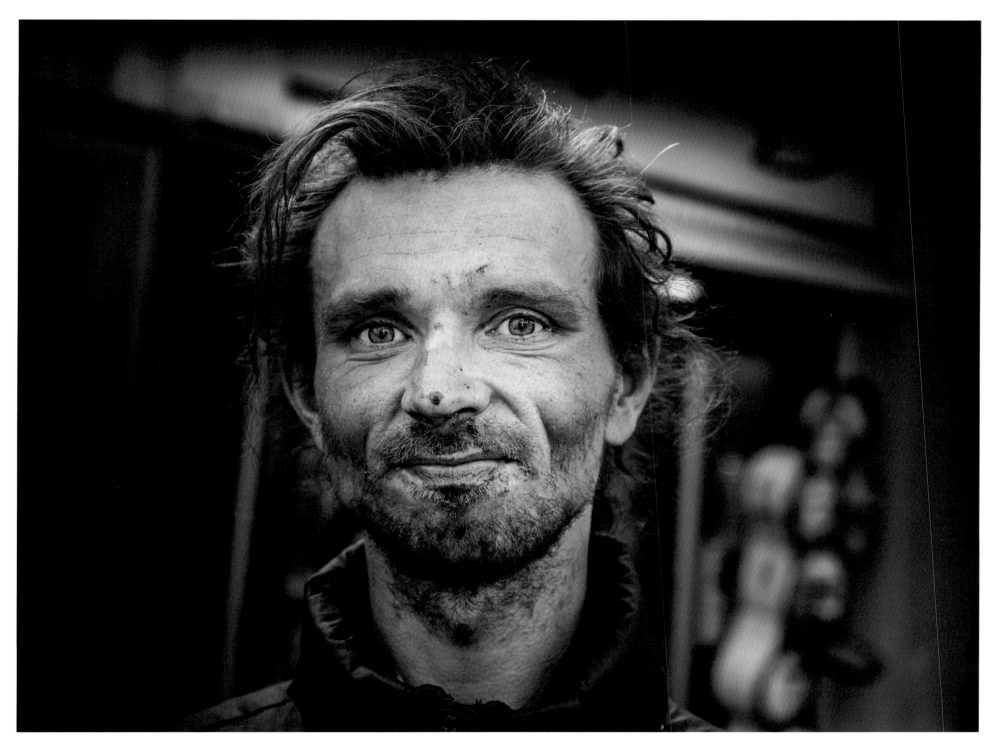

SEAN BRESSENDEN PLACE

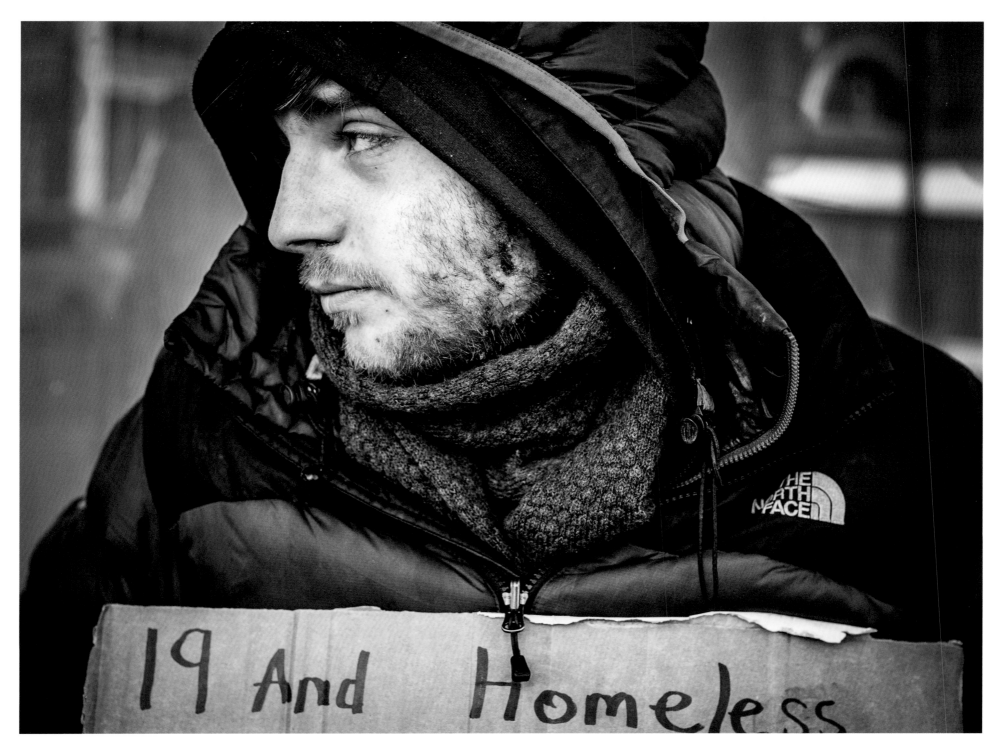

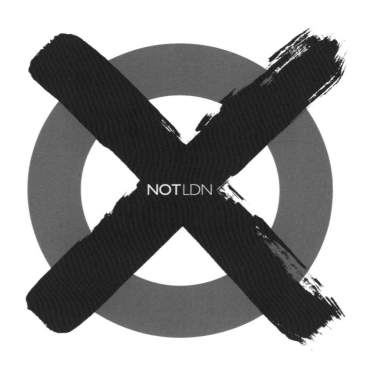

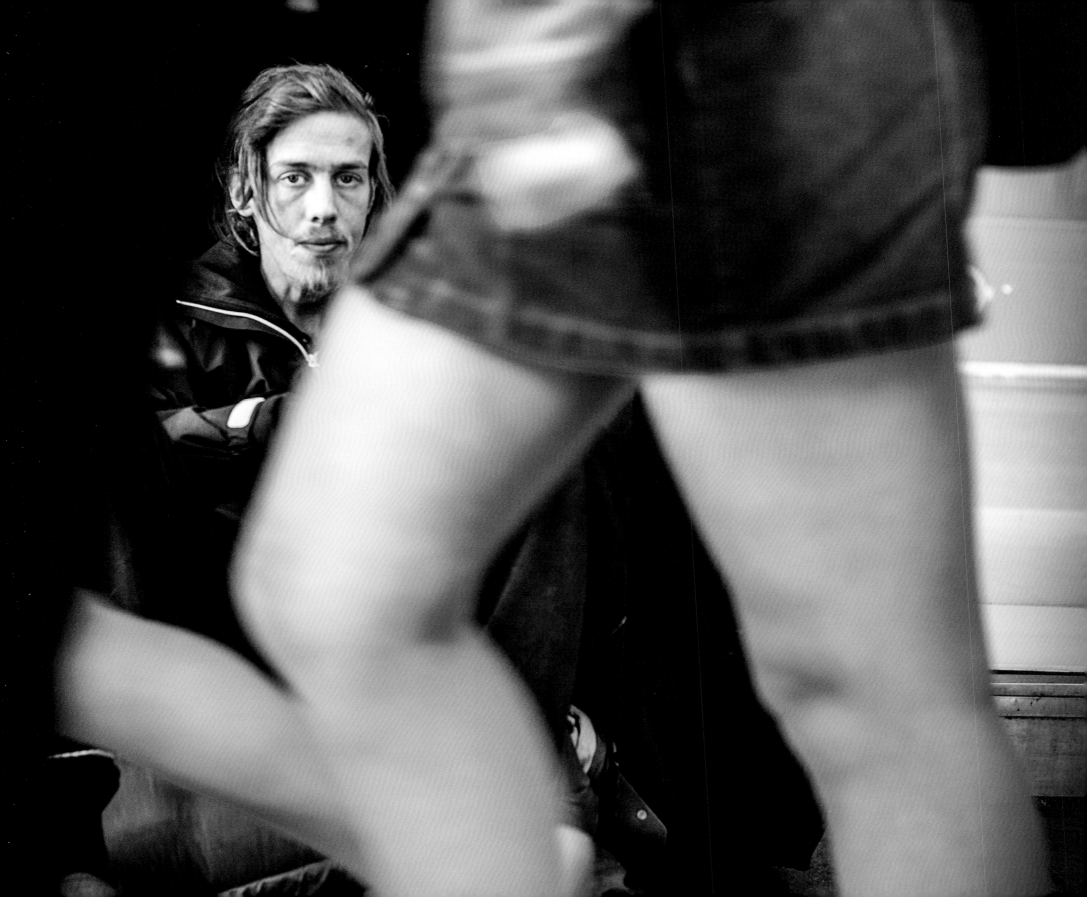

<< **TOM** VICTORIA STREET / **CHRIS (& ZEUS)** PICCADILLY >

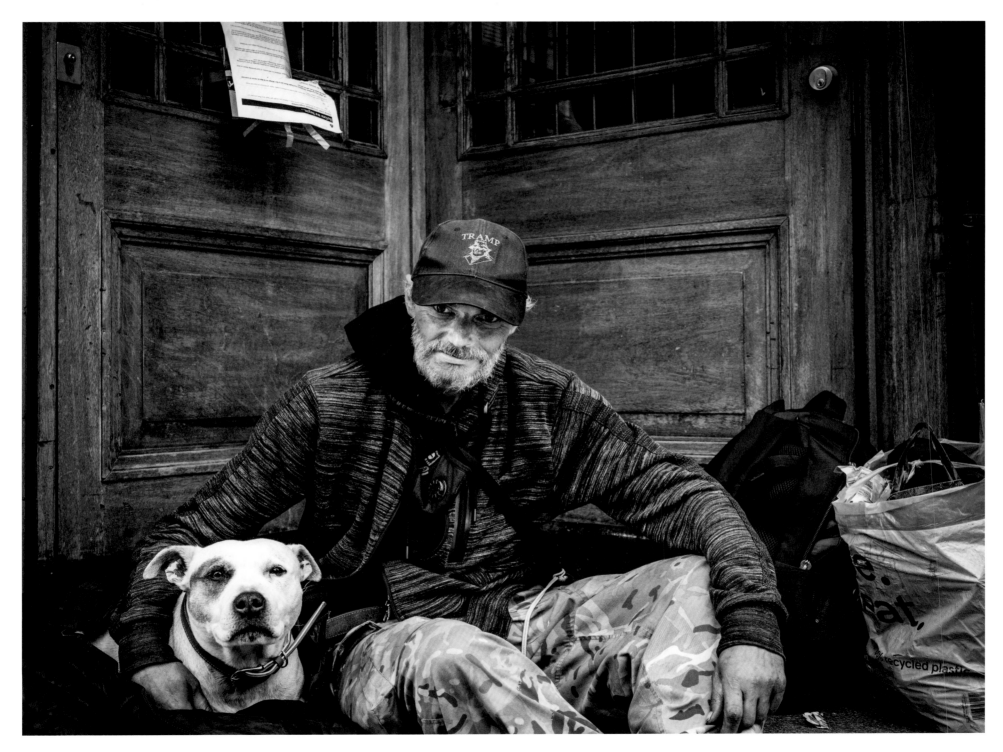

STEVE BRESSENDEN PLACE

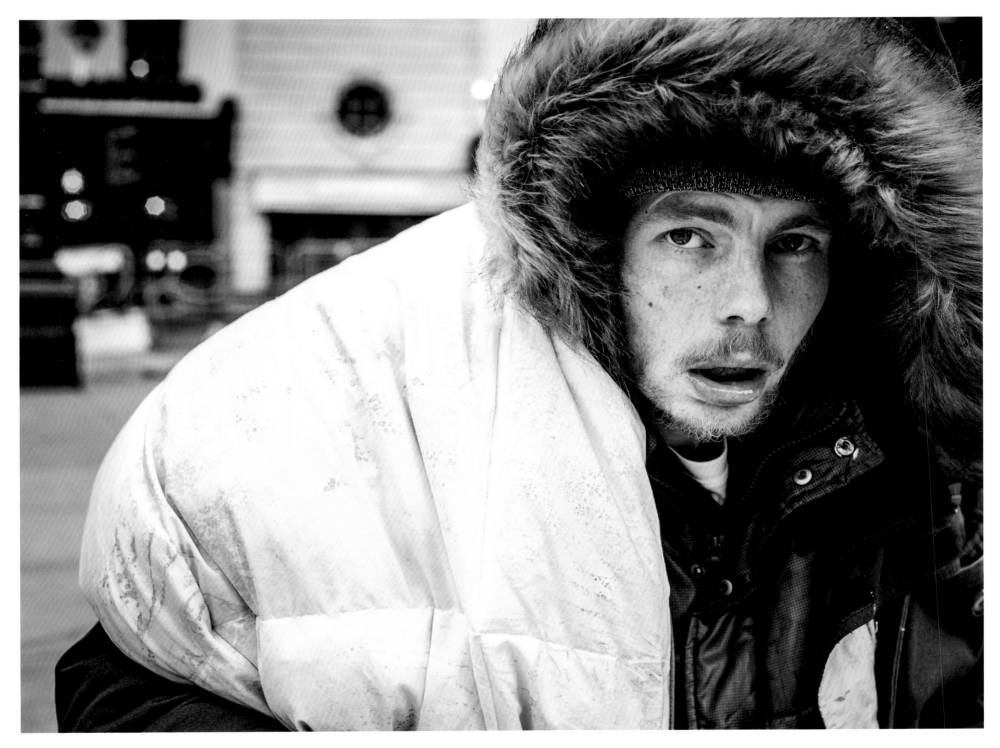

NICK RUPERT COURT

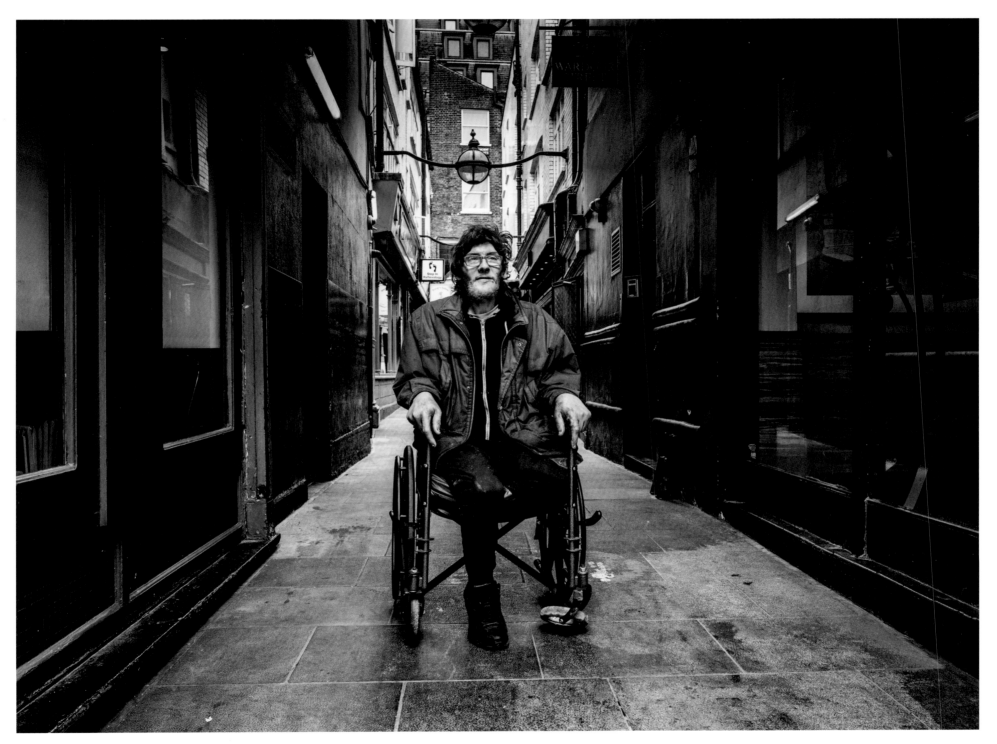

SOPHIA EARL'S COURT ROAD

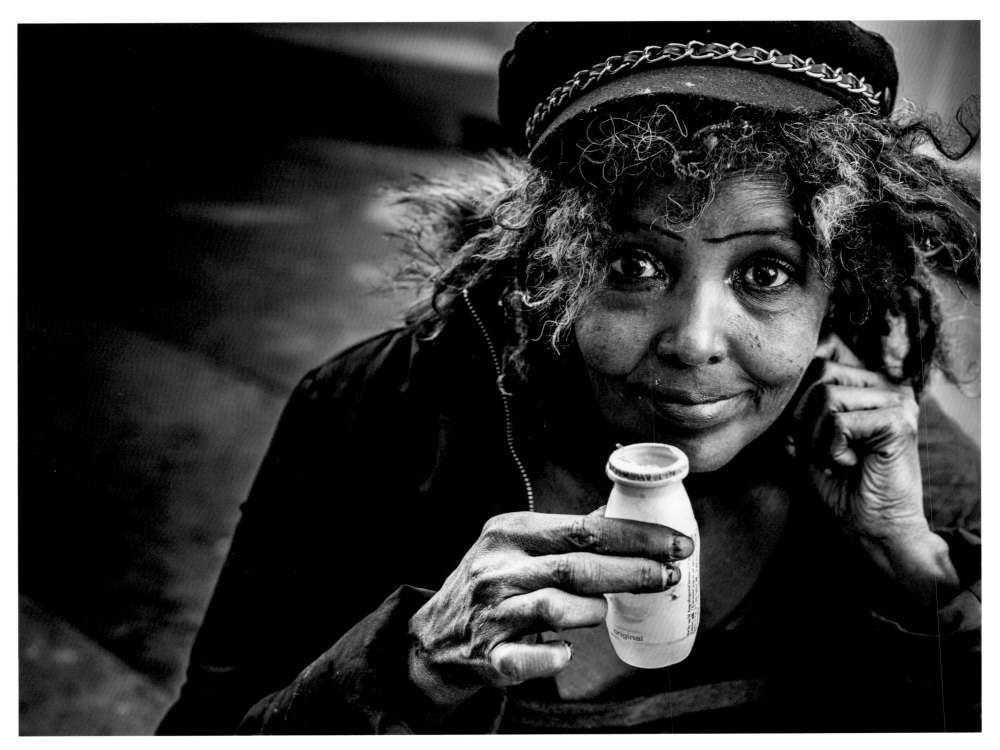

ANON VAUXHALL BRIDGE ROAD

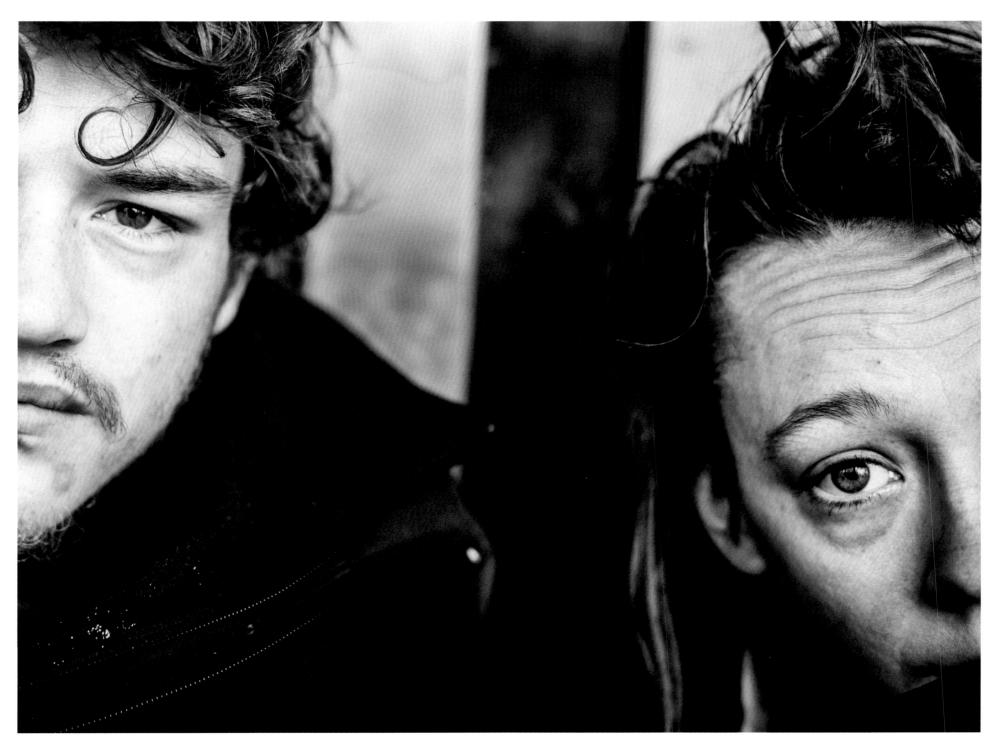

NICK CHRISTOPHER GARDENS

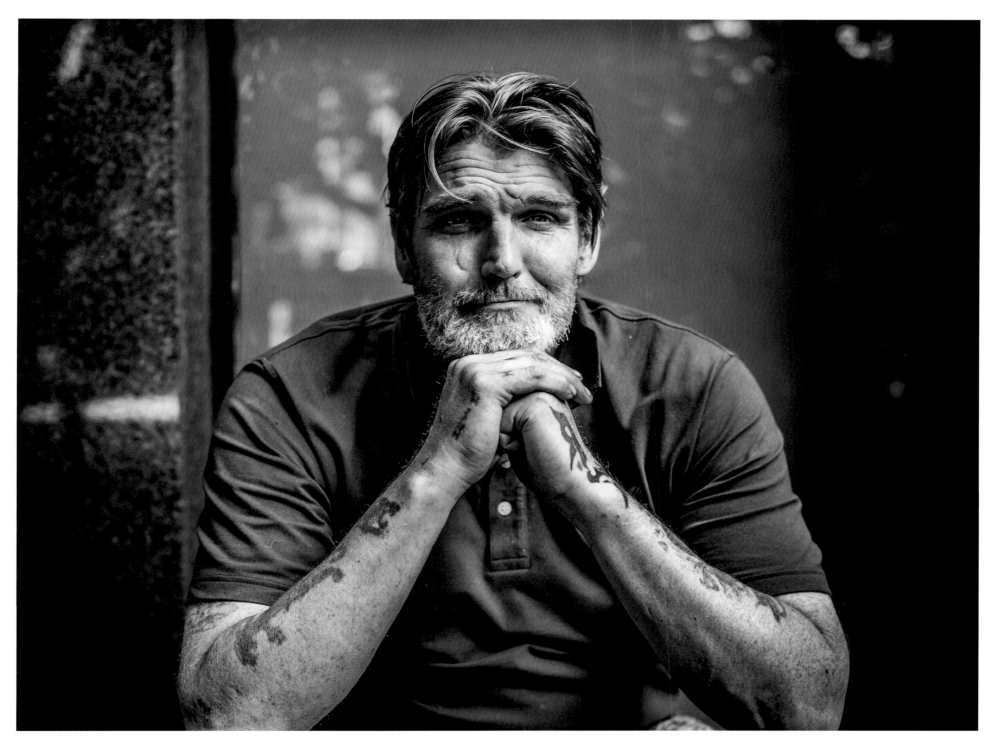

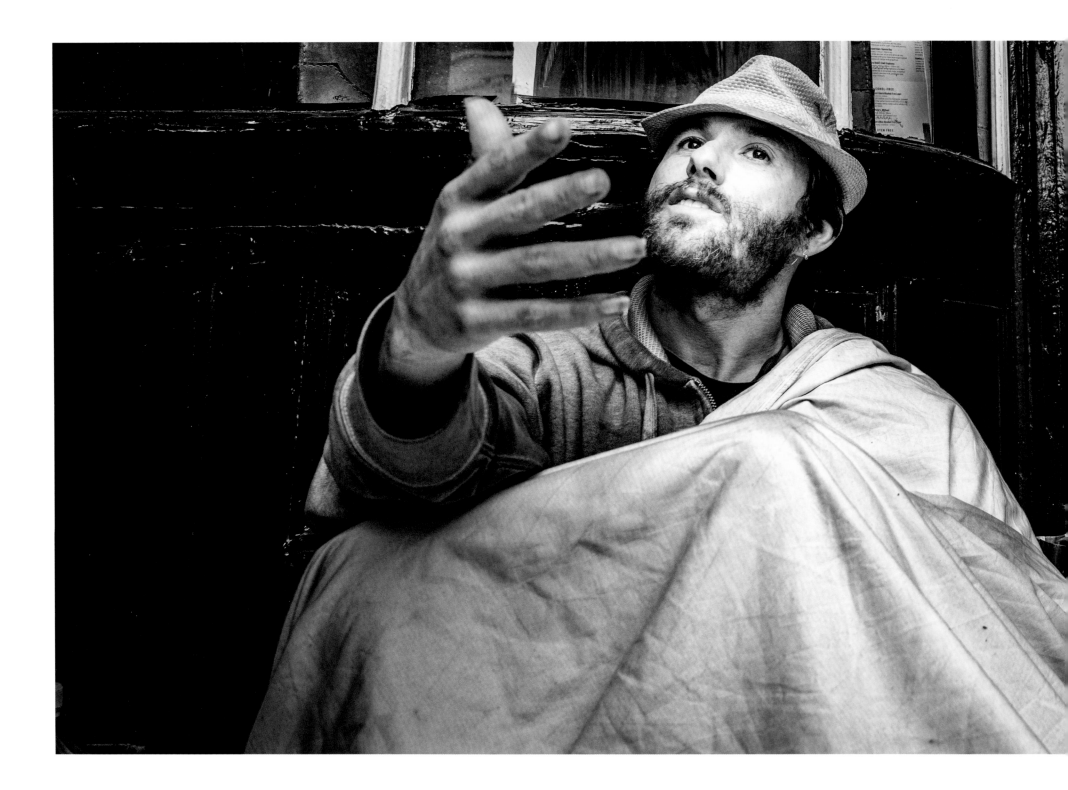

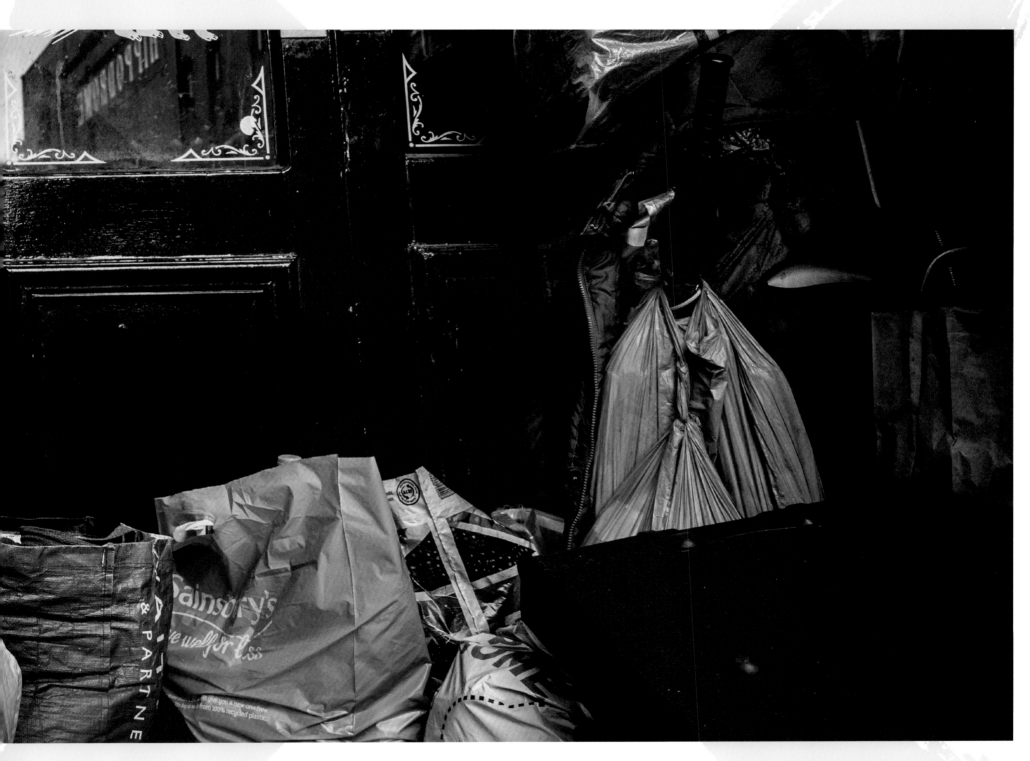

<< **ARTUR** CHARING CROSS ROAD / **EMMA & CJ** VICTORIA STREET >

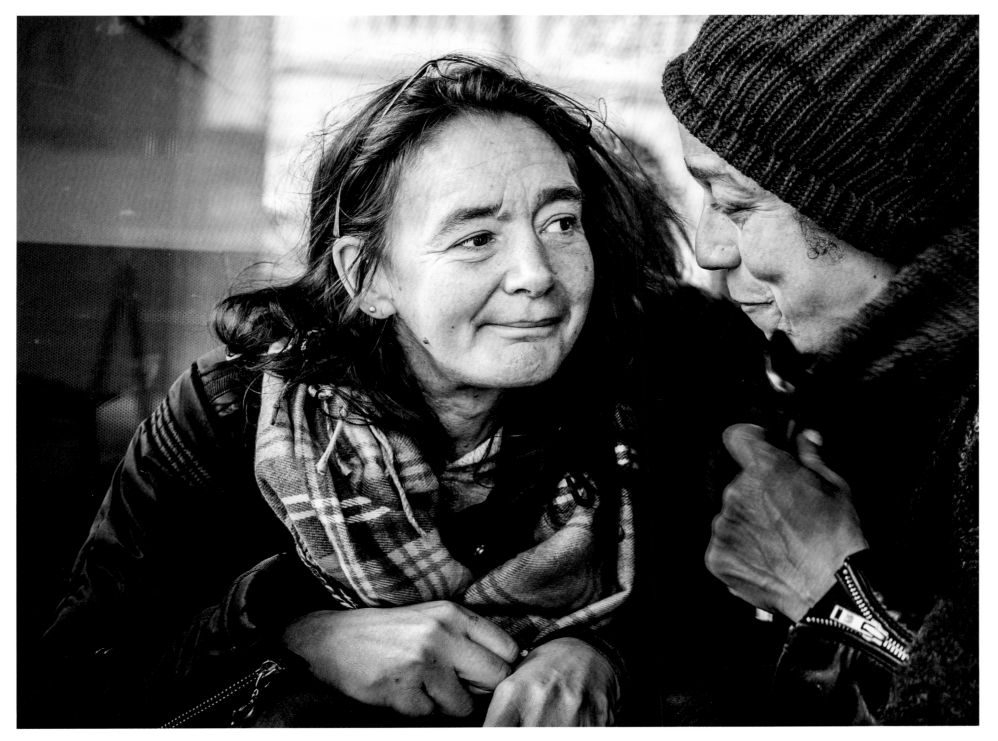

ELENA GROSVENOR GARDENS

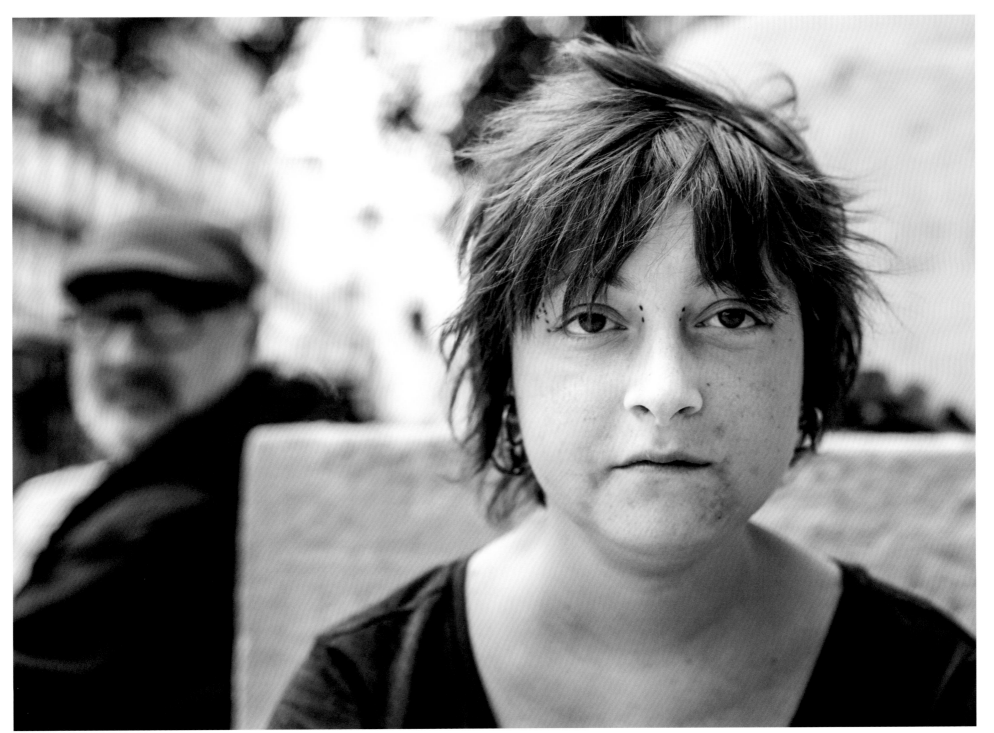

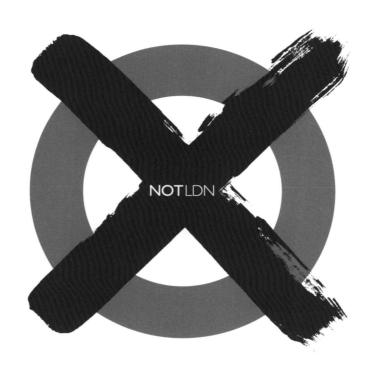

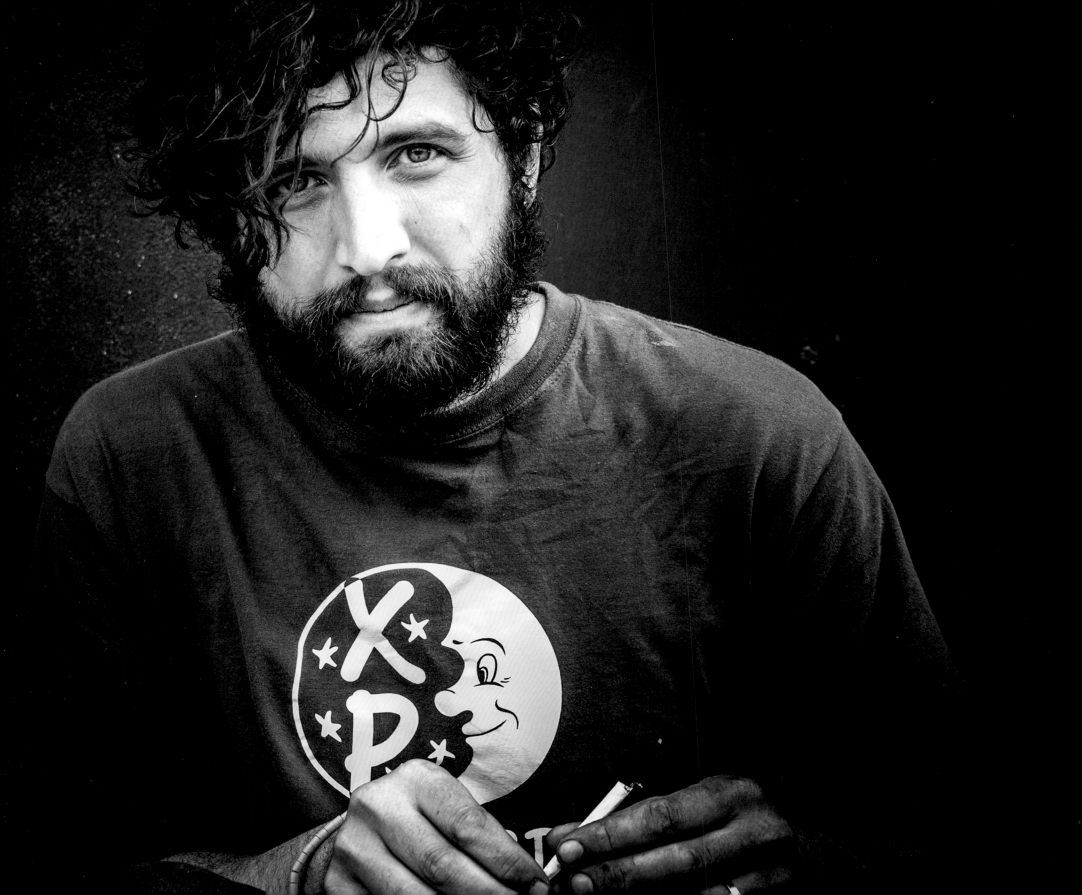

<< **JOSEPH** EARL'S COURT ROAD / **ANON** CHARING CROSS STATION >

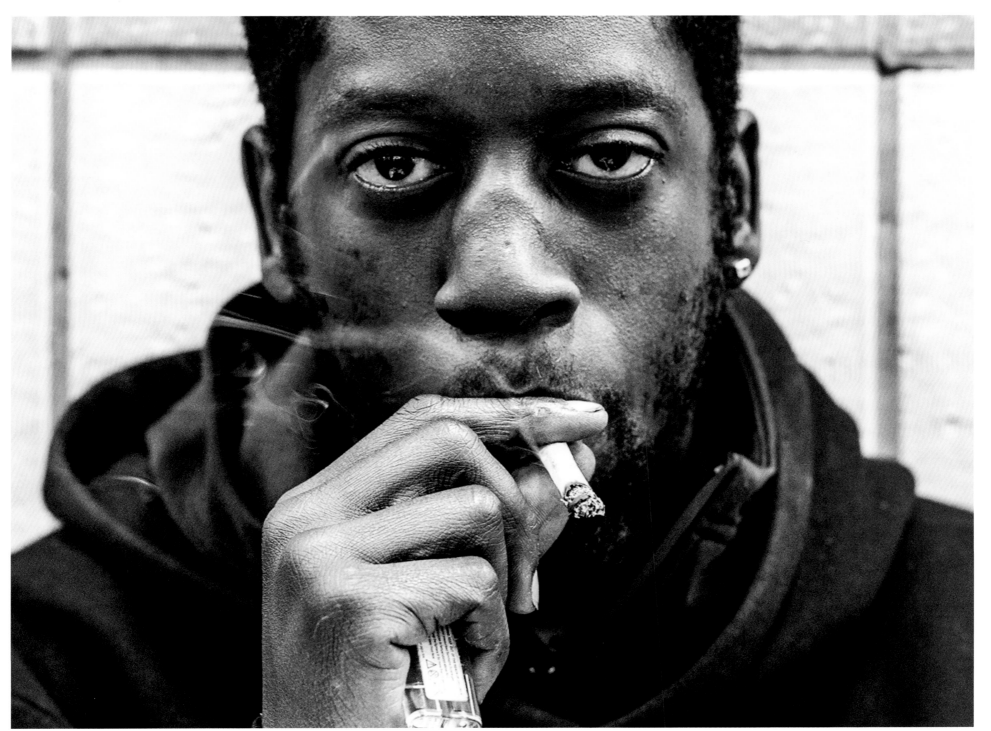

ANON CRAVEN STREET

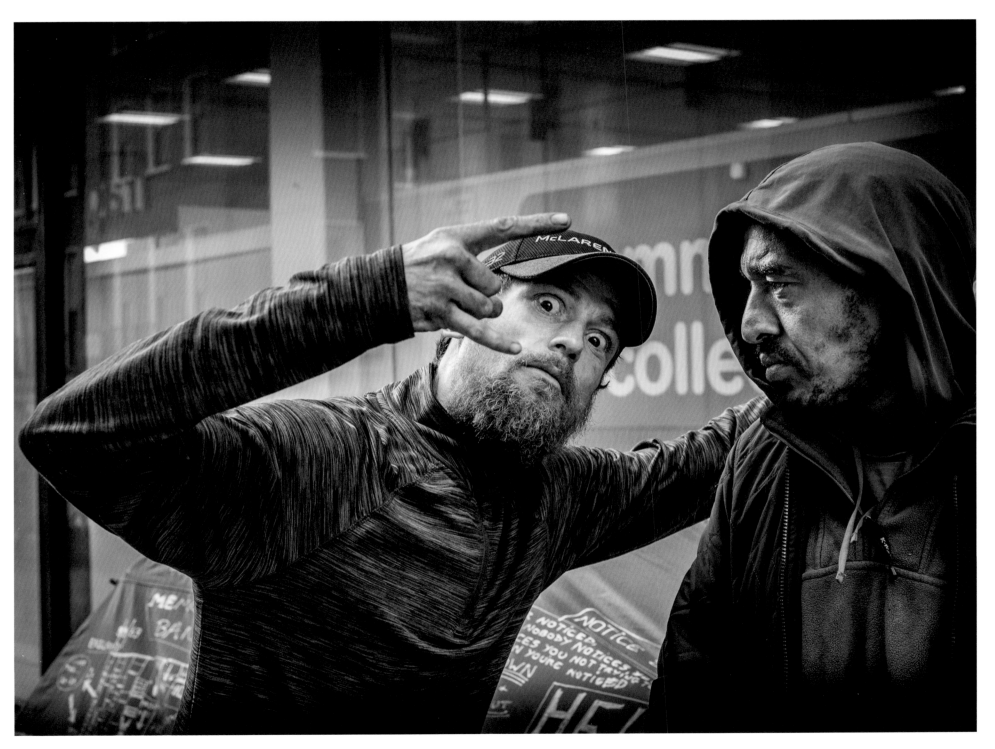

MARIE VICTORIA STATION

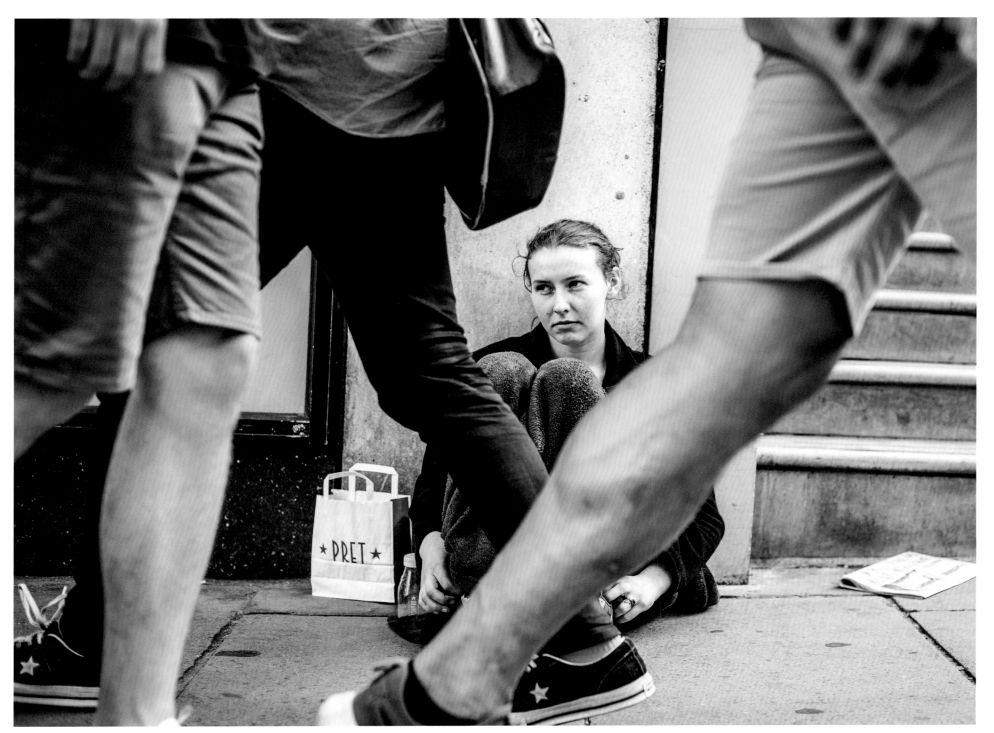

TANGO & CHRIS GROSVENOR GARDENS

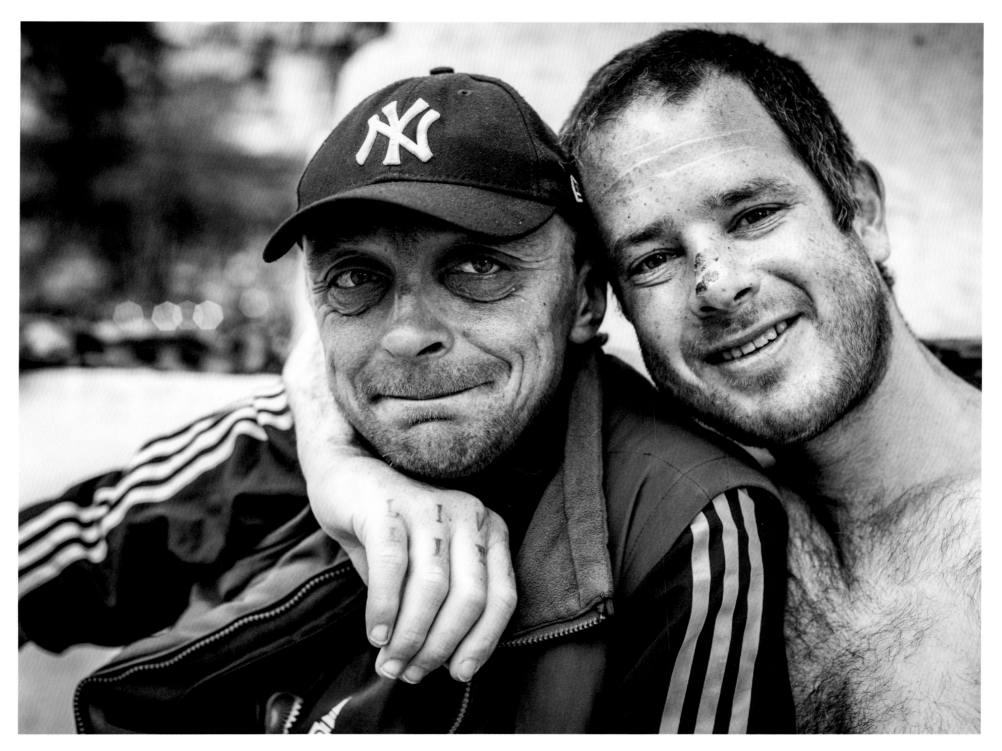

MICHAEL CARLISLE PLACE

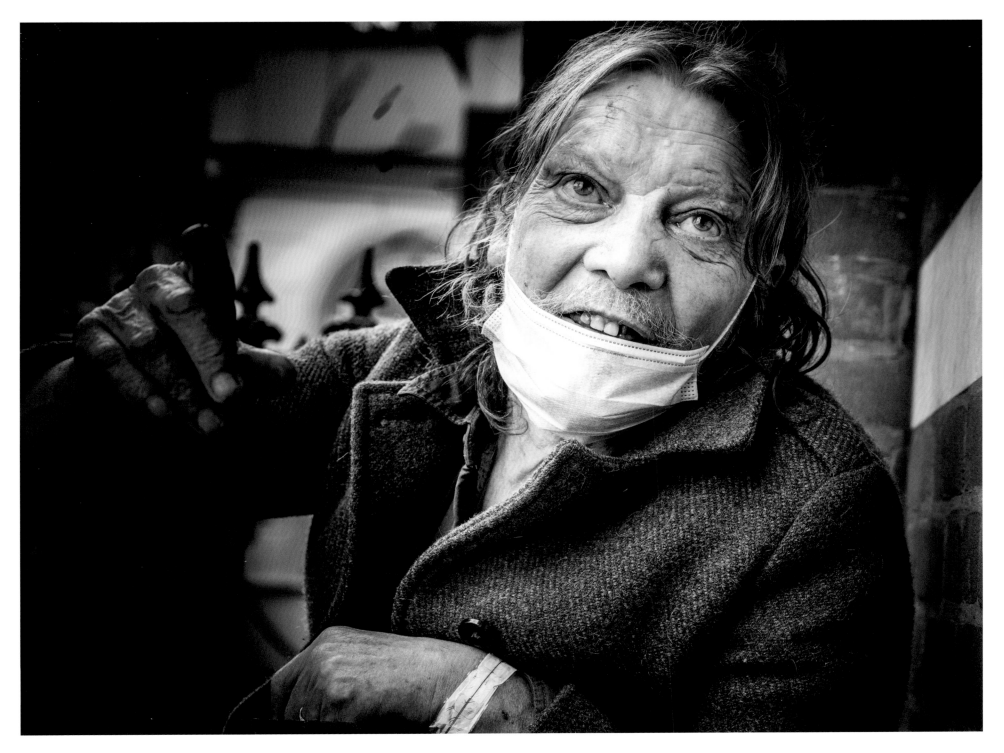

DAWN VICTORIA STREET

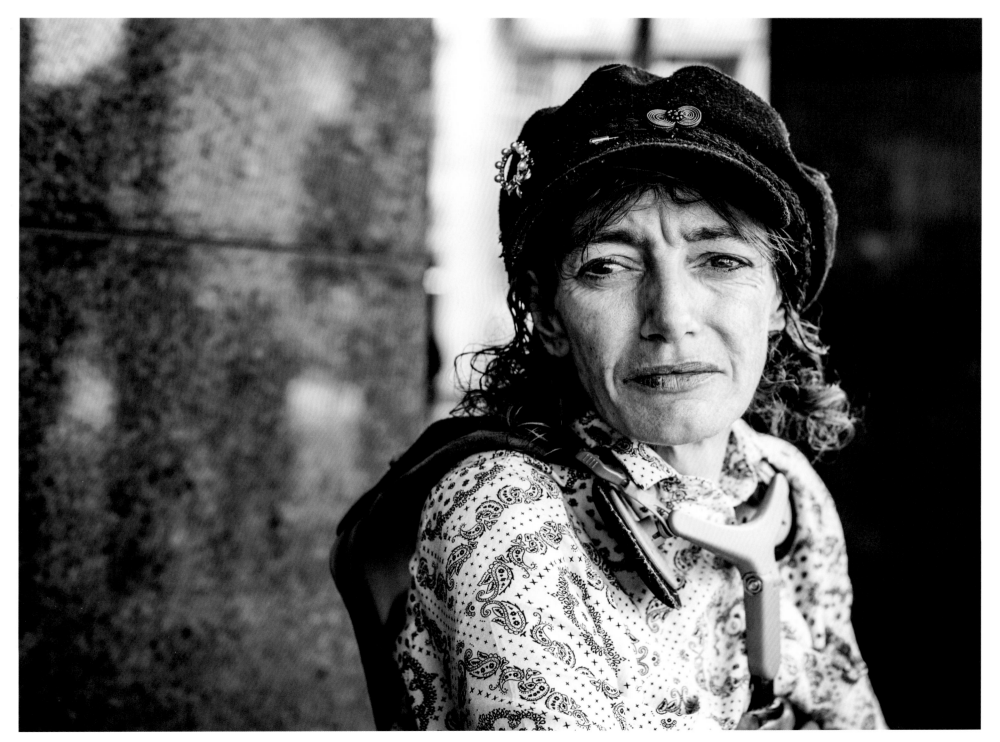

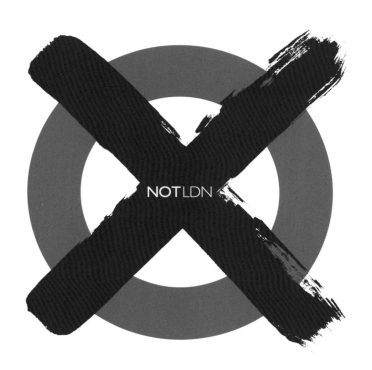

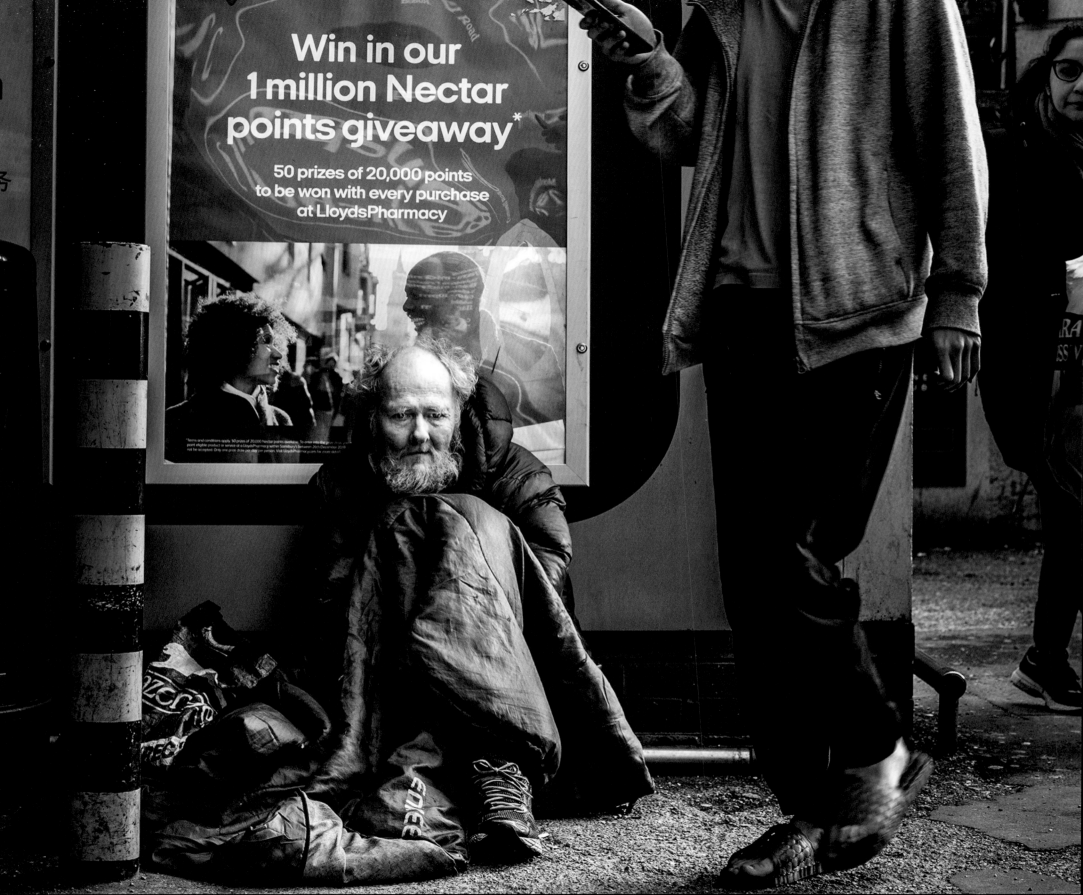

<< **CHRIS** CROMWELL ROAD / **TONY** ASHLEY PLACE >

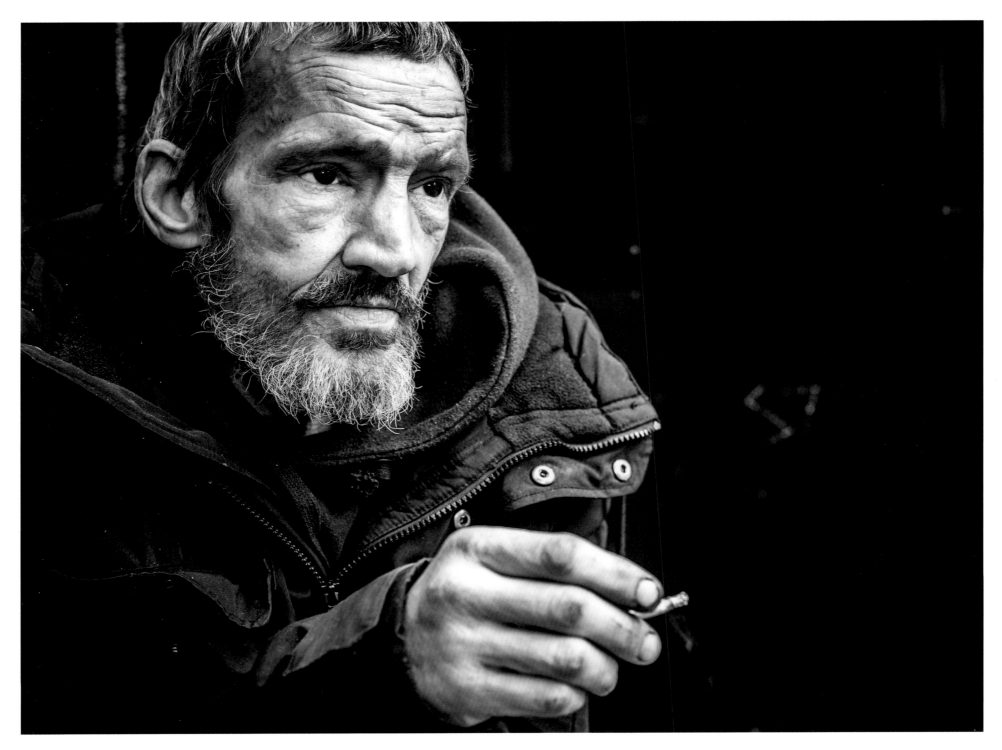

GARY VICTORIA STATION

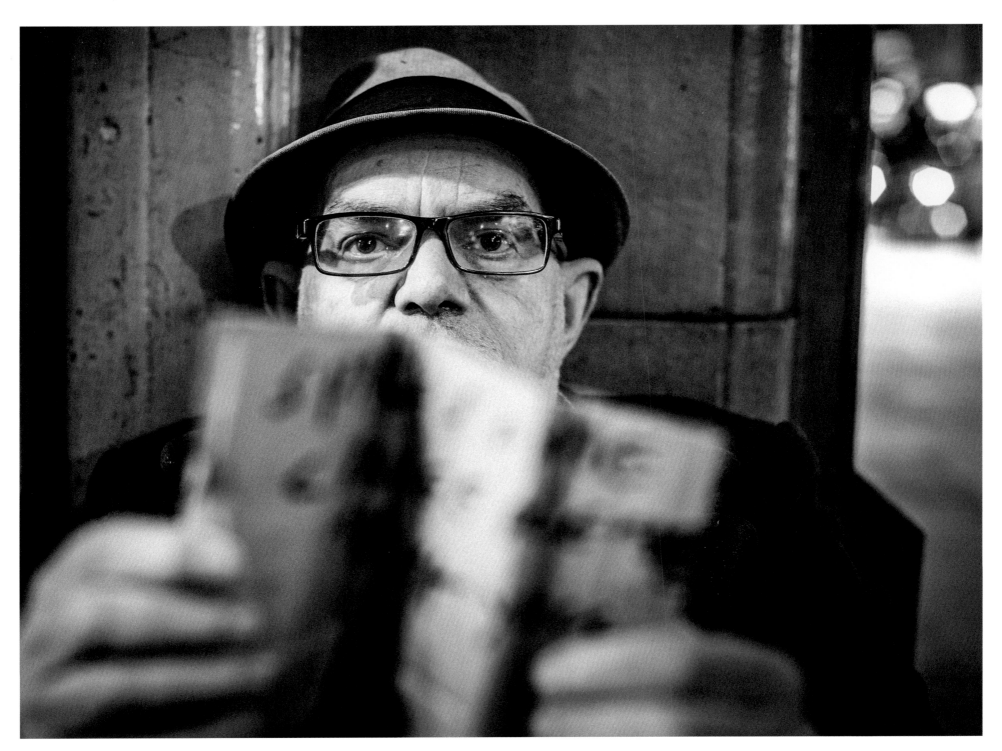

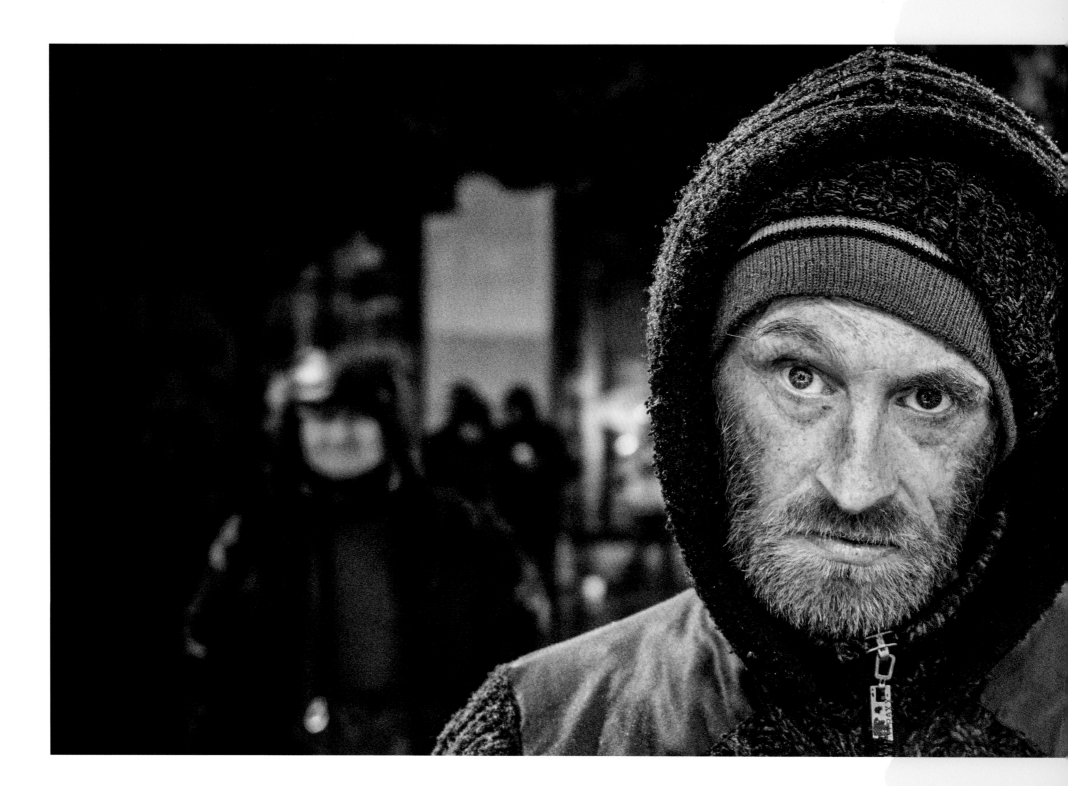

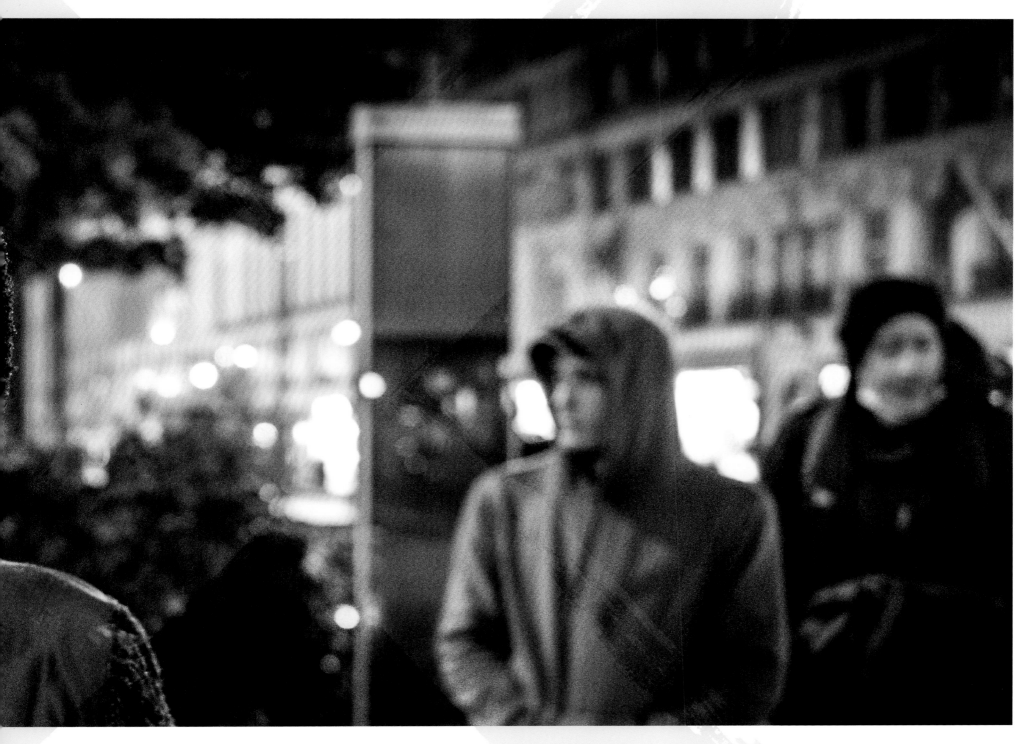

<< **ANON** WILLIAM IV STREET / **GEORGE** WILLIAM IV STREET >

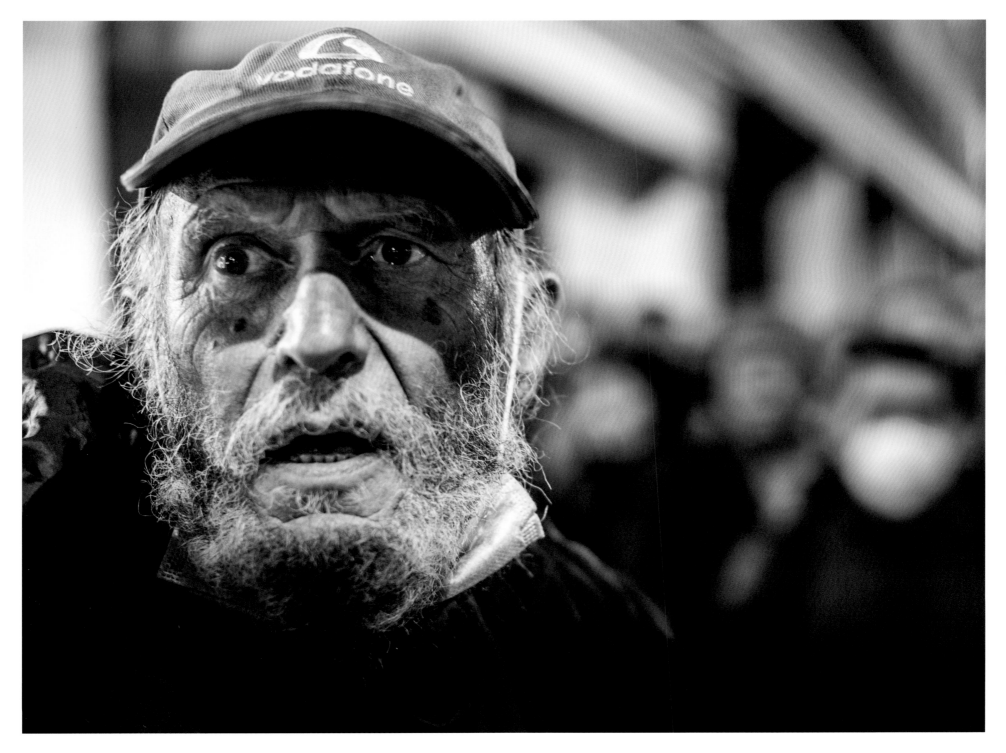

ANON CHARING CROSS STATION

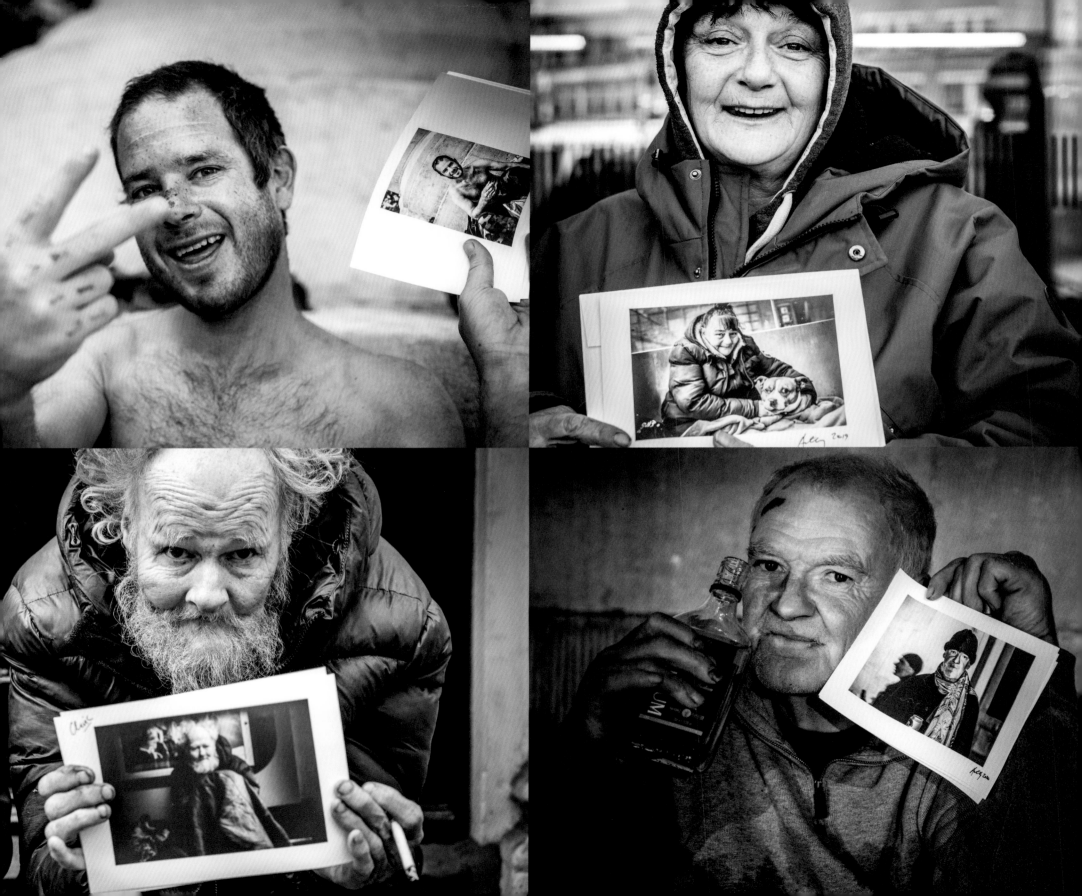

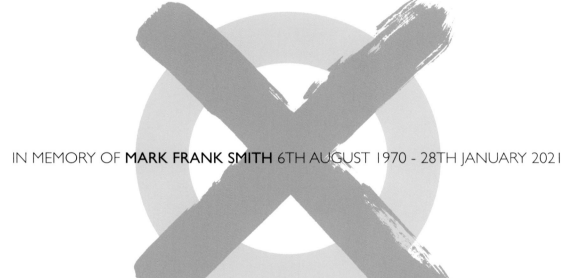

IN MEMORY OF **MARK FRANK SMITH** 6TH AUGUST 1970 - 28TH JANUARY 2021

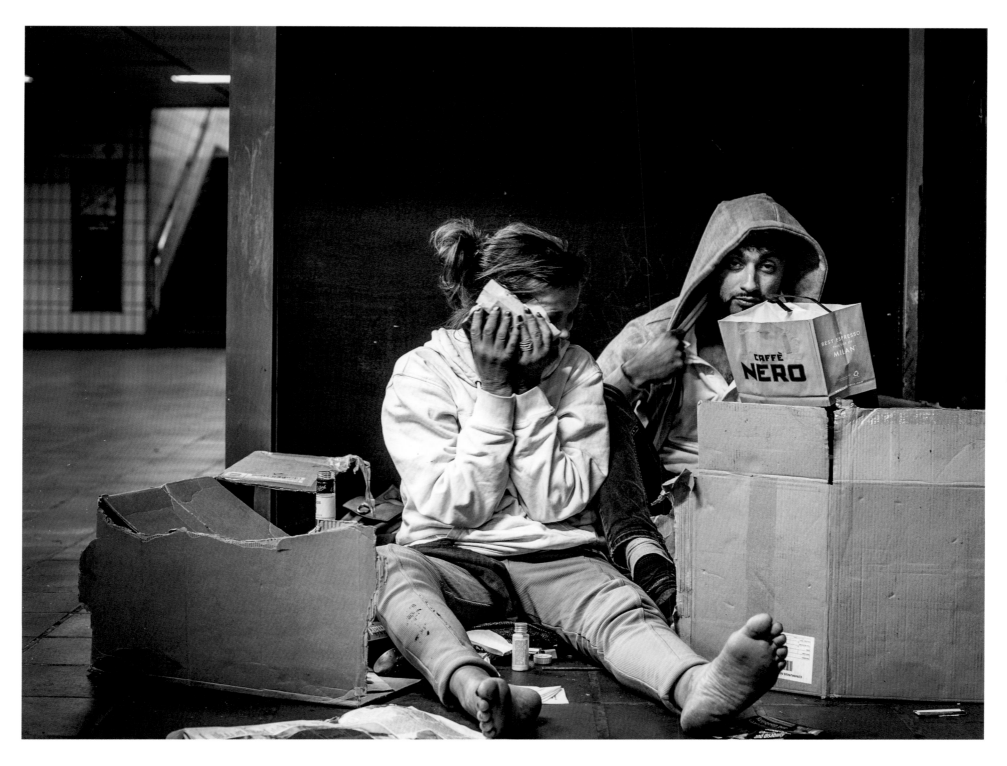

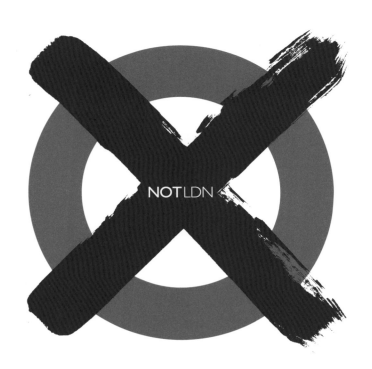

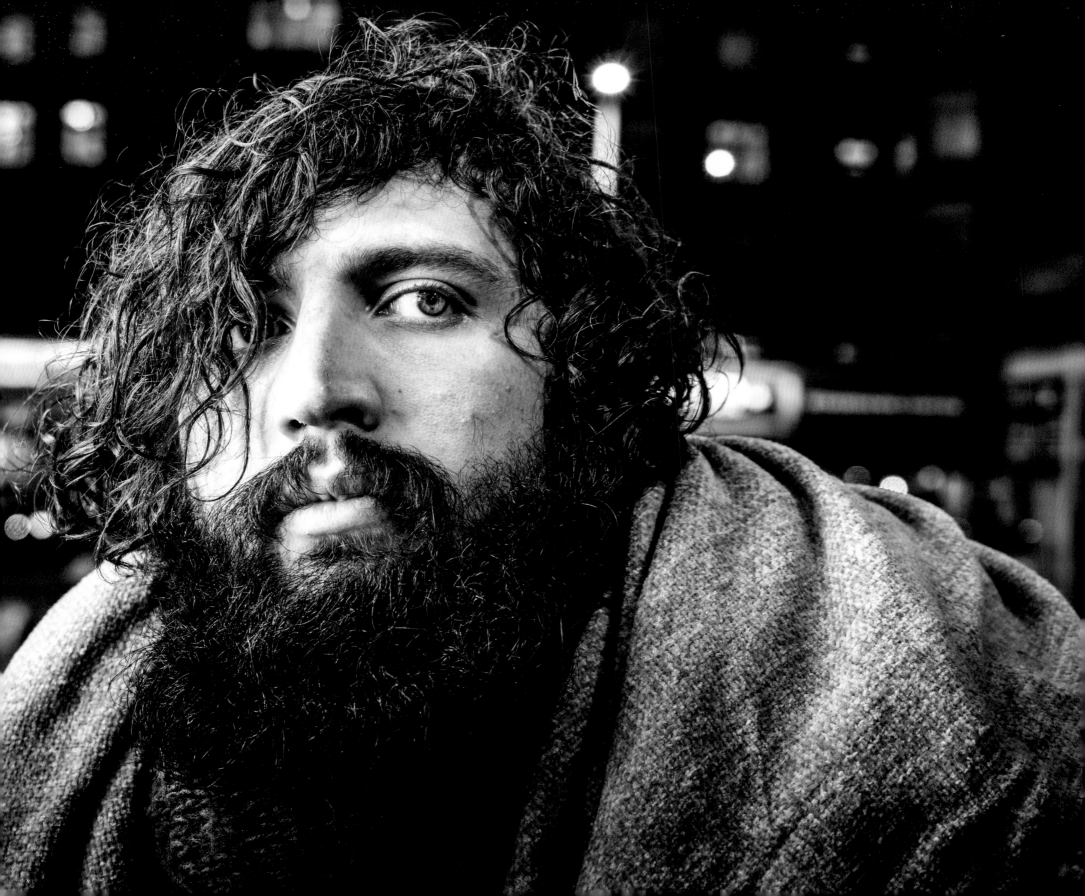

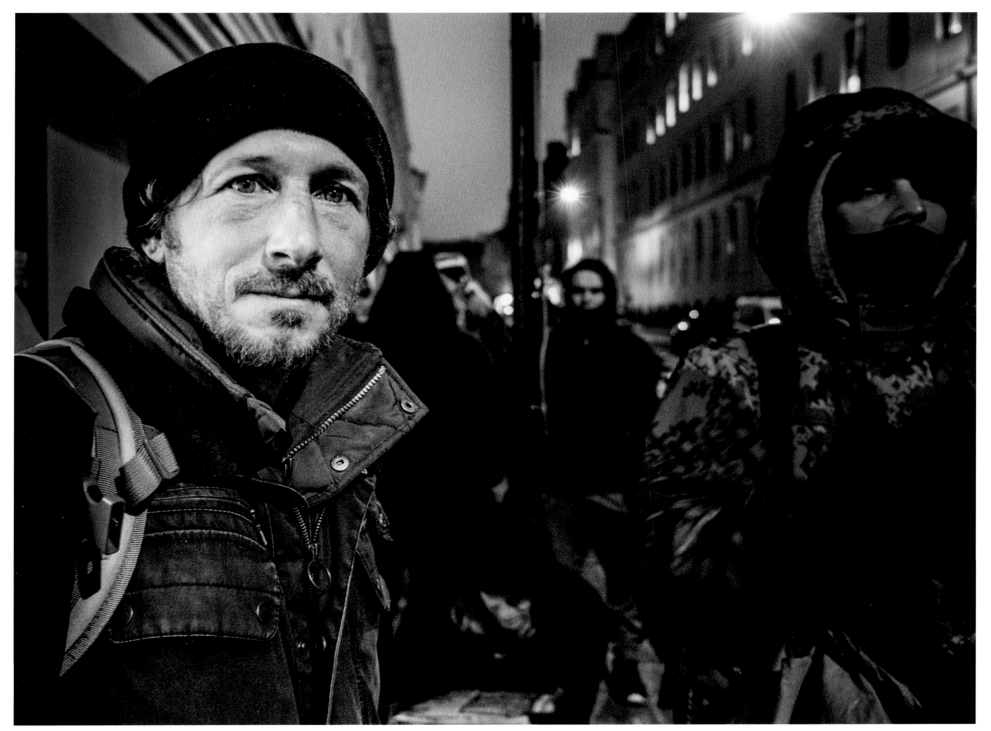

MICK ST. PAUL'S CHURCH, COVENT GARDEN

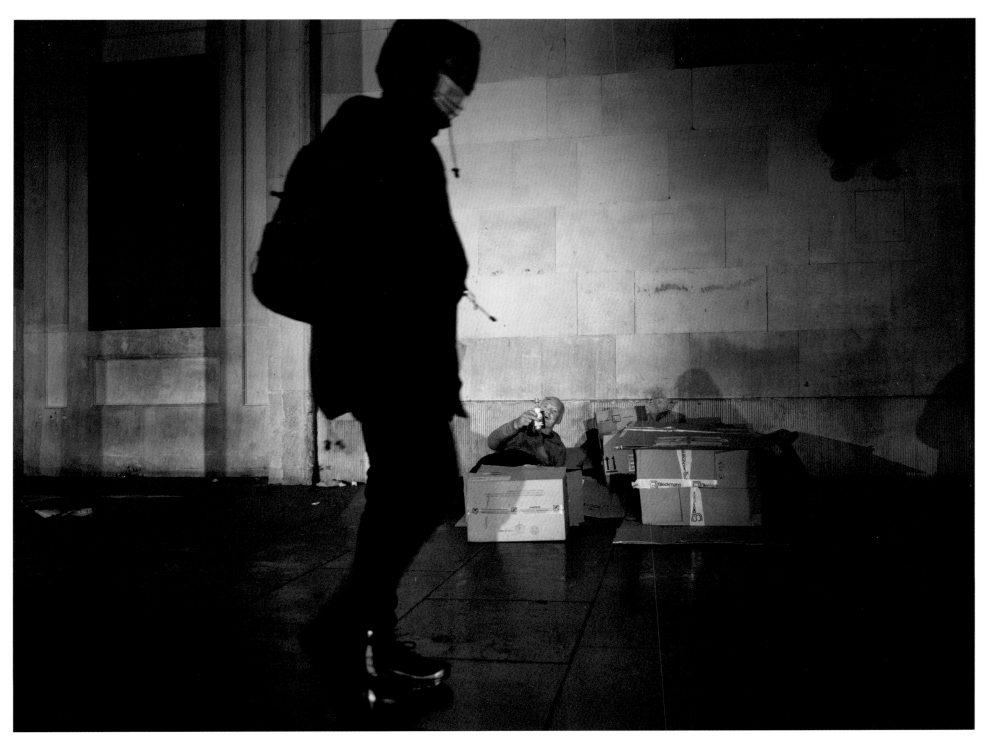

DANIEL BEDFORD STREET

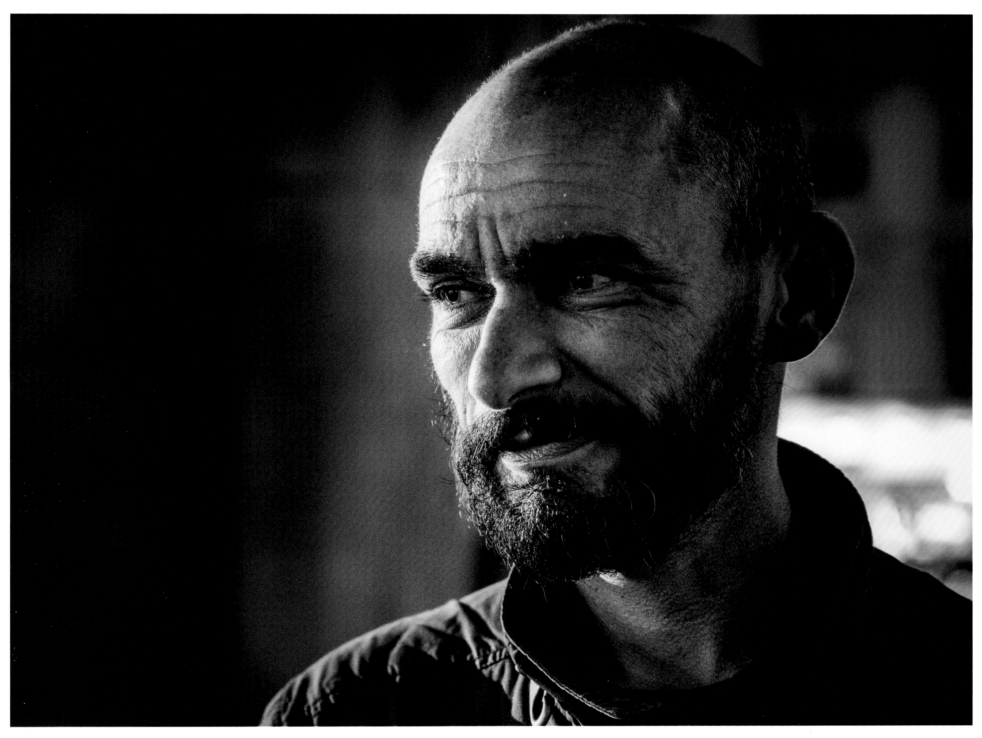

BILL SOUTHAMPTON STREET

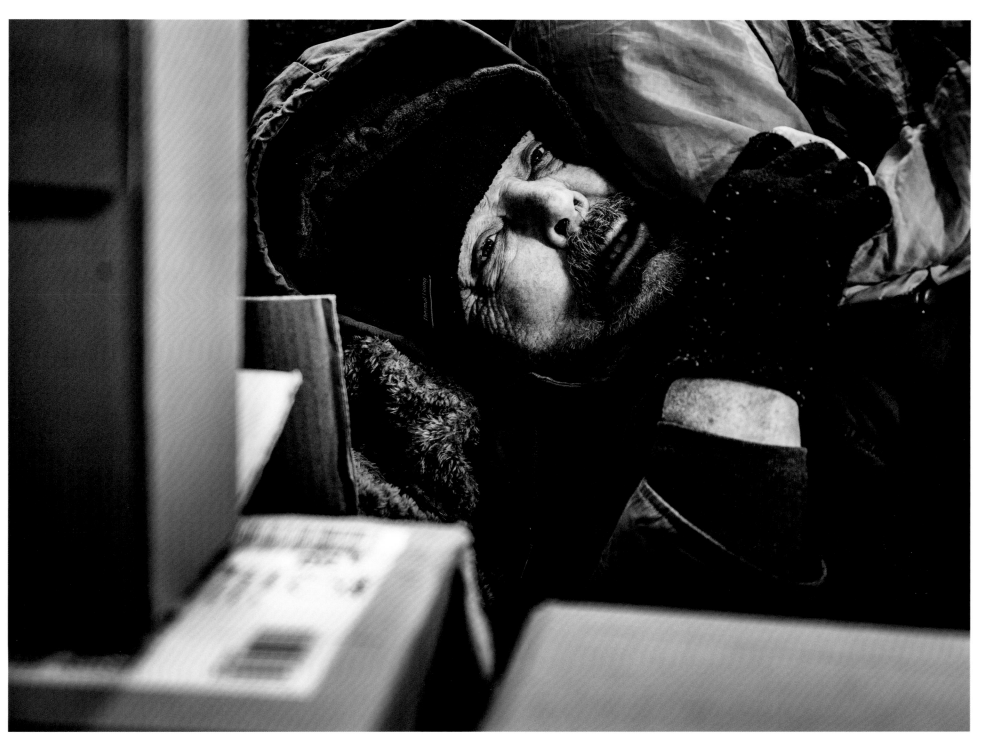

ALICE EARL'S COURT ROAD

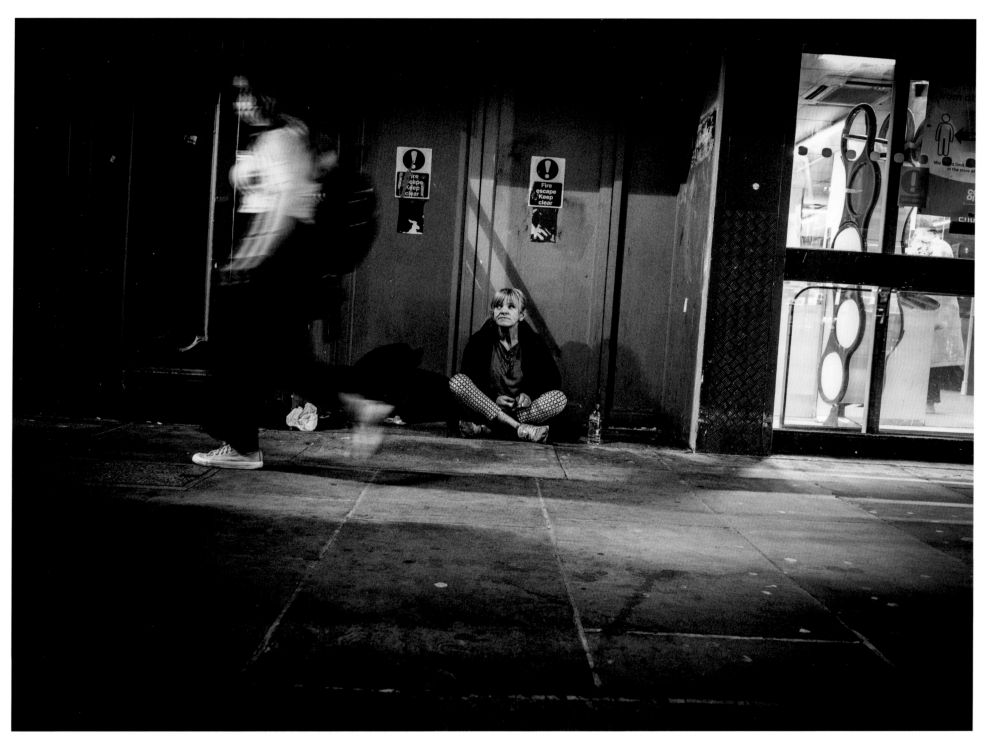

PAGE 5 The first person I photographed for the project. Just outside Liberty's department store. She was Polish, she and her boyfriend had to come to London to work in the hospitality industry. They had started taking drugs and lost their jobs. The boyfriend had managed to get back to Poland but she was now a heroin addict and neither could not or did not want to go back. She was desperate to shake the habit but she didn't know how.

PAGE 9 This is Vincent! He sits on the streets of South Kensington during the day and sleeps in virtually the same place at night. His aim is to raise enough money each day to get a bed in a hostel. I saw him in the rain and then in the snow with little to protect him. He said he had been on the streets for four years. He said he never knew his family and had been in orphanages and in care homes until he was an adult. He said he would love to have a job to get out of all this.

PAGE 11 This is Amy and her dog Fleur. Reluctant to be photographed at first because she said she was a mother with five children. Her mother was now looking after the children while she was on the street. I wish we had talked to her more.

PAGE 15 Photographed in a most mundane location, I was struck by the timeless look of this woman.

PAGE 17 Ben, 43, has been homeless for 14 years. Originally from Romford, he used to live in Finsbury Park. He said he was not offered accommodation during Lockdown, despite having outreach workers. He said it was very quiet with no one around but kind people offered food. I commented on his bright green sleeping bag which he said was lovely and warm but he had only had for two weeks. Ben told me his mother died when he was 13 years old. His father remarried. He said his Dad does what he can to help him. He said he would love to get off the streets but said there was no accommodation available. He told me he always goes to Crisis at Christmas.

PAGE 19 This is Kingsley, originally from Sierra Leone. He came to the U.K. via Holland and has been here for 21 years. He told us his mother had become a heroin addict and when his father died, he left home.

PAGE 23 Denise. We called her the Bird Lady. She sits on the pavement up and down Piccadilly and lived on the large grass roundabout at Hyde Park Corner where with bright coloured balls and food, she had attracted several, virtually domesticated parrots, flying around her seemingly as though welcoming her return.

PAGE 29 Mark. Over the eighteen months of the project, we would see Mark nearly every time we were in the area. He was kind, thoughtful and helpful. But with increasing frequency he would disappear for days consuming vast amounts of alcohol. All those around and caring about him; Raoul the 'Big Issue' seller, his sister in Scotland and P.C. Leo Chapman whose 'beat' Mark was on had all warned him that he was going to kill himself. It was all to no avail. On 28th January 2021 Mark was found dead… The last time we saw him was with P.C. Leo Chapman who was on his final beat telling the homeless in his area that he was leaving the police. In tears Mark quickly wrapped a 'present' and gave it to Leo. When they embraced, I thought for a moment that this might be the beginning of a new start for Mark. I was wrong.

WHO?

PAGE 31 Hayley and Dean. She said she had been on the streets for three years. There was no family to go back to. Her 'mum was on drugs.' Dean did have a place in a hostel nearby but spent his days on the streets and had done so for years. I was struck by the warmth of the relationship between them. She called Dean 'My beautiful pudding'!

PAGE 37 Rebecca, South Kensington Tube station. She had been homeless for three years when we first met her. She told us a boyfriend threw her out of their flat. She had weak knees and said she was taking methadone. She sold newspapers to avoid being moved on for begging.

PAGE 39 Anonymous. Spice is the bane of the homeless. He told me, 'it is the way we get through the cold, it's the way we forget things.' He reckoned the stuff was 'government sanctioned'. He said that if I had an exhibition, he would like to write next to his photograph what he wanted out of life, in regard to what his ambition was. He said that it was to make money to stop the next generation of his family becoming alcoholics and homeless. Two sisters had committed suicide, the rest of the family were alcoholics, and he felt the kids were going to go the same way. He wants to start a dog-walking business.

PAGE 43 Jovita from Lithuania and Marco from Italy. She was living in Devon for three years working for a holiday flat-letting company in Woolacombe Bay. The contract ended and she told us she was then 'a victim of a robbery in Barnstaple.' She said she was in London trying to sort out papers and her life and had been sleeping rough for two months. She is pictured with her boyfriend Marco. He had worked on a cruise ship. A job that broke up his marriage. He wants 'to go to Margate and work in entertainment.'

PAGE 51 Sean, as it states on his placard, is 19. His father died when he was a baby. His mother 'got depressed' and turned to alcohol and drugs, committing suicide when he was eight. From then on, he told us, he spent his childhood in various foster homes. He had a place in the YMCA but was sharing with a 'kiddie fiddler'. He had to get out. He thought he had been on the streets for about six weeks.

PAGE 53 Tom. I had photographed him before but did not recognise him. At that time, he had been on the streets for a month or two. He was heartbroken. His said his boss had gone off with his girlfriend. Since that time he told me he had been in prison. He broke into a shop and stole clothes and just hung around for the police to arrest him and put him in prison, where at least he was warm and fed. Today he is freezing and shivering.

PAGE 55 This is Chris and his dog Zeus that Richard had met the day before. He is wearing a cap advertising the nightclub Tramp that he says he is proud of and was given to him by someone with a Lamborghini! Of concern was that he told us over the weekend he had been attacked by up to a dozen people who had kicked him and his dog and stolen the dog's bedding and his phone and wallet.

PAGE 57 I had photographed Steve, the traffic-cone player twice before. He sings into the traffic cone to get money! The first time I came across him he was full of energy and chatty, six months on there has been a change, he has become distant, disengaged and lethargic. I noticed it took him ten minutes to open the packet of biscuits he had with him.

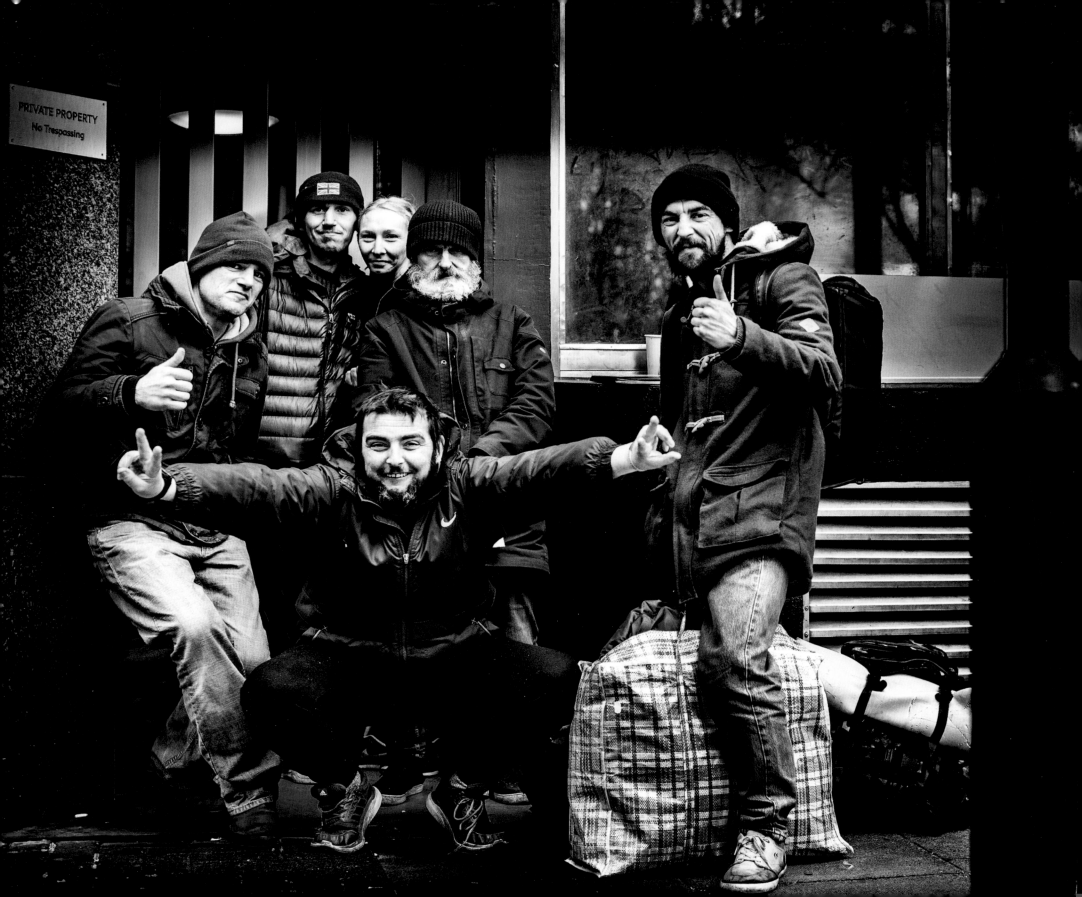

PAGE 61 It's late afternoon and Sophia is sitting in the middle of the newly barred off part of the road outside the Co-op in Earl's Court. She is being given food but does not ask or seem to want money even though she says she has to beg until the end of the week when she gets 'paid' her benefits.

PAGE 65 Nick. He says it is not important where he comes from. His father died whilst he (Nick) was in hospital. His brother and sister are in Cardiff but he 'lets them get on with their lives' but says he keeps in contact with them. He was pleased that Prêt-a-Manger gives them all free drinks. He told us he likes photography and used to have a Canon camera. He took my picture with my camera.

PAGE 67 Artur (not Arthur). Charing Cross Road. He is Spanish from Alicante but has been in the U.K. for ten years, four or five of which have been on the street. This pub entrance is where he sleeps as well as where he 'lives'...

PAGE 69 Emma (left) & CJ. Emma has been on the streets for 4 years. CJ said it had been longer for her and admitted to being 'too attached to alcohol'. They said they occasionally get a place at a hostel but found them mostly unhygienic with rats and mice. Next to them, out of shot (but appearing on page 31) is their friend Dean, who seems less engaged than Emma and CJ.
A sad moment was when the women recognised the photograph of Hayley (with Dean on page 31) in my portfolio and said that she was a friend who had died a couple of weeks ago.

PAGE 71 Elena, an artist from Spain trying to get back there. She did!

PAGE 77 Never got his name, but he was hyperactive and very proud of his tent. I went back a few days later to give him a print and see how he was. The area (Charing Cross) was surrounded by police. Someone had trashed his tent. He was yelling, shouting and inconsolable at what had happened. I hung around to make sure he was not badly dealt with by the police. In fact, the opposite was happening, they were doing their best to calm him down.

PAGE 79 Marie from Glasgow. She suffers from epilepsy but told us 'medication keeps it OK.'

PAGE 81 Chris is from Cumbria. The day we first photographed him he had a sore nose from too much sun. He was very pleased with the subsequent print of himself which he said he would send to his mum who did not like him being on the street, but he thought it would show her that he was well and happy.
He said many outreach social workers helped and one had promised to replace his lost mobile. His friend in the cap told us that he was Polish and had a job.

PAGE 83 Michael has a walking frame due to a car accident he had eight years ago. The driver did not stop. He goes to the Passage for one meal a day, breakfast and for the rest, he says he lives on fags and booze. He told us he was homeless. He has a wife but they seem to have drifted apart. He is engaging, humorous and clearly well read.

PAGE 85 Dawn is wearing a neck/back brace and is in a wheelchair. She had been kicked in the back while sleeping on the street. Recently I was pleased to meet her with her outreach worker. She had recovered and was walking unaided.

PAGE 89 Tony. He told us he had 'been on the streets forever.' That he was born in Westminster to Irish parents. He told us he had been in and out of jail all his life but had gone straight for four years. He said he doesn't drink a lot, but smokes a bit of cannabis. He said he slept on the bridge at the back of Victoria Station.

PAGE 91 Gary is Tony's friend (see previous photograph and note). The cardboard notice in his hand says: 'Spare some change please, Thank you.'

PAGE 95 This is George the 'philosopher and book reader'. Here he is at the front of the food queue on William IV Street. We had met earlier in the day. He sits on a bench opposite the National Portrait Gallery with a pile of books next to him. We discussed Shakespeare, Chaucer and Bernard Shaw amongst other luminaries.

PAGE 97 She holds a toasted sandwich to her cheek for the warmth. Even sheltered in the Underground it gets very cold. I am glad they had each other for company. They were clearly struggling.

PAGE 99 Joseph. It was a bitterly cold day and Joseph was clearly suffering but still trying to get enough money to find a place to stay. The time was approximately 9pm. I have met him several times since this photograph around mid-December. He wants to write about his experience on the street and contribute to this book.

PAGE 101 The food queue, William IV Street.

PAGE 105 Daniel, 39, suffers from COPD and says he is an alcoholic. He told us he left the Navy 15 years ago. His last posting was for four years on submarines. He then went AWOL as he disagreed with the U.K.'s involvement in the Iraq war. He was caught and says he was put in a cell for four days and sprayed with cold water every time he tried to sleep. He had recently been in a hostel but was evicted for having a bottle of vodka.

PAGE 107 Bill was a lollipop man from Plumstead. He told us he had left the marital home after a split with his wife and had been homeless for 2-3 months. Soon after we took this picture, we heard he had got into temporary accommodation to where we sent the photograph. He replied that he had put it up on his wall as 'a pleasant reminder of a dark and dismal time'!

PAGE 111 Some days they cheered us up…

WHO?

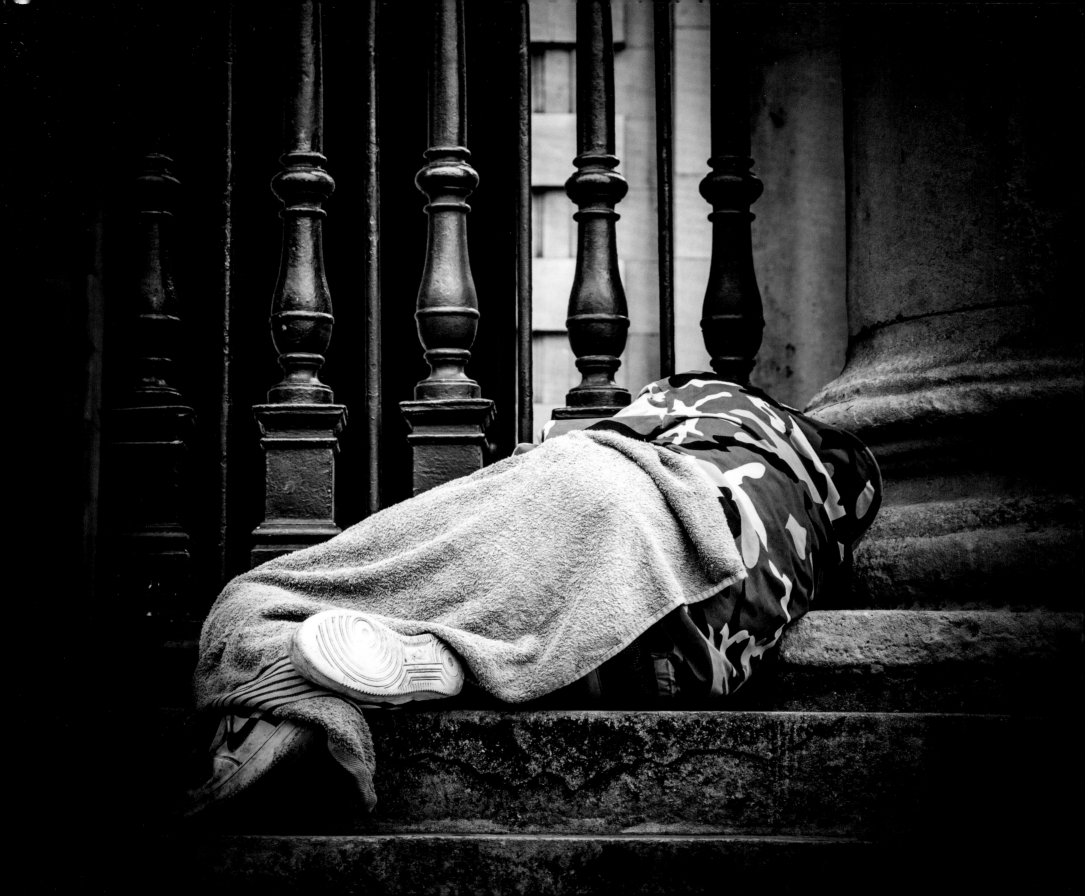

With every photograph I took I asked the question whom am I to step into this person's life and take a photograph. Subsequently I have been confronted again with this question as friends and colleagues 'proof read' the 'manuscript'. For the record, no photograph was taken without permission preceded by an explanation of why we wanted to take a photograph. I always promised to come back with a print the next day and some of the loveliest moments in the nearly two years of the project were seeing the joy of my subjects having a 'professional' photograph of themselves to keep. But I hope the above explanation is redundant in the light of the photographs themselves: a collaboration between the photographer and the subject. An attempt by me to say something of meaning, or at the very least to give pause for thought and for them to tell their story.

A brief CV

2009 UNICEF / Al Madad project in Niger

2009 Exhibition at Sony World Photographic Awards, Cannes.

2010 Australian CCP exhibition - toured South East Asia for twelve months.

2005 - 2012 main contributing photographer to the The Silent Witnesses book series; 2005 Silent Witnesses, The Lives of Palestine's Children.
    2006 Kashmir's Children, The Silent Witnesses of the Earthquake.
    2008 Desert Faces, The Silent Witnesses of the Niger Drought.

2015 Zaatari Refugee camp on the Jordanian/Syrian border for Save the Children and Said Foundation.

2018 Photography for the Kayani Syrian refugee camps and schools, Bekka Valley, Lebanon.

2018 Photography and film for the Kanafani Foundation, Beirut and other regions in Lebanon.

2019 - 2020 NotLondon project.

Influences: Lewis Hines, Eugene Smith, Michael Duane and Jim Goldberg amongst others.

METHOD